"I highly recommend this book!"
-Professor Paul Wood AO

DR. ELIZABETH PRITCHARD AND CHRISTINE BURNS

THE AUTHENTIC LEADERSHIP PLAYBOOK

STEP INTO YOUR POWER. OWN THE ROOM. REDEFINE THE RULES.

ISBN: 978-1-969463-95-2

Table of Contents

Introduction

Who Is This Book For?

This book is for you.

Regardless of your role, title, or who you think you need to be to qualify as a leader, true leadership has nothing to do with your job description. It begins and is ultimately defined by how you lead yourself.

This playbook is your invitation to embrace a powerful truth: Every one of us is a leader, and the first person we are called to lead is ourselves.

Without self-leadership, we wouldn't accomplish a single thing each day. From getting out of bed to achieving our daily goals, self-leadership is essential and ever-present. From the toddler who is exploring their likes, dislikes, and learning self-control, to the oldest and wisest person on this planet, we are continually leading ourselves.

This journey of self-leadership is where true influence begins. It's where we discover who we are, uncover our passions, tap into our internal drivers, and amplify our innate strengths. Through this process, we learn to inspire and uplift those around us. Not by position, but by presence.

This is Authentic Leadership. Powerful, real, and available to every one of us. When you choose to lead authentically, you create ripples of impact that reach far beyond your immediate circle, influencing people of all ages and walks of life.

This book is designed for busy professionals who are ready to lead more effectively. It's built on decades of evidence-based insights, powerful stories, and the lived experiences of the authors, Elizabeth and Christine. Over the years, we've seen firsthand how Authentic Leadership produces extraordinary results.

Inside this book, you'll find simple, practical, and energizing strategies that work. You'll be able to apply one or all of them straight away into your work, your sport, or your personal life, and experience immediate shifts. With courage, confidence, and clarity, you'll step into your power as an Authentic Leader, unlocking breakthroughs and creating results that truly matter.

What Is Authentic Leadership?

Elizabeth

Let me share a story that illustrates the power of Authentic Leadership.

A few years ago, I worked with a manager named Sarah to help her develop her Authentic Leadership skills. Sarah was known for her transparency and genuine concern for her team. She always took the time to understand each team member's strengths and aspirations.

When her organization embarked on a $2.3 million grant submission, Sarah was tasked with leading a complex, high-stakes collaboration involving multiple departments, two countries, and tight deadlines.

At first, she reverted to her familiar pattern; taking control, checking every detail, and making most of the decisions herself. The pressure to succeed was immense, and despite her best intentions, the team began to feel stifled. Meetings grew tense, creativity faded, and collaboration gave way to quiet competition.

That's when Sarah recognized the cost of overcontrol (you might think of it as micro-management) and decided to lead differently.

One day, during a particularly challenging stage of the project, through our coaching, she shifted her approach. Instead of dictating solutions, she encouraged open dialogue and empowered her team to generate innovative ideas. She created space for learning from mistakes and set the tone for ingenuity and experimentation. Her authenticity built trust and collaboration where every team member had each other's backs, embraced accountability, spoke with candor, and consistently completed milestones ahead of schedule.

Sarah's Authentic Leadership not only helped her team meet the deadline with time to spare, but also inspired each individual in her team to embrace their own strengths and authenticity.

Christine

Sarah's story is a powerful reminder that high performance isn't about pushing harder, achieving more, or burning yourself out in the process. It's about *alignment*: Bringing your values, purpose, and mindset into congruence so that what you do each day reflects who you truly are.

Authentic Leadership is the catalyst for this alignment. It invites you to lead from the inside out, with clarity, courage, and confidence.

In my decades of working in elite sport and high-performance environments, one truth stands out: performance without authenticity is temporary. When leaders operate through control, perfection, or comparison, they limit what's possible - for themselves and their teams.

But when they lead with authenticity, they build trust, spark creativity, and unleash collective excellence. That's when results become sustainable, meaningful, and deeply rewarding, for the leader, their team, and everyone they influence.

Redefining What It Means To Lead

As you delve into the information and practical applications within this book, you might think, *I don't have the time or energy to learn a different way of being a leader.* Or maybe, *Leading with authenticity is just another fad in the business world that I can ignore.* You might even think, *If I do what I really want to do, aren't I being self-centered or egotistical?*

These concerns are valid to some extent, but they are the outcome of patterns that we have learned in life (which we explore more throughout this book) that have led you to where you are now.

You are reading this book because you know there is a better alternative. A more effective way of leading. A more powerful way to enlist your incredible strengths and rise above the limiting beliefs that hold you back.

Let us show you why limiting beliefs do not support the Authentic Leader in any way.

Inspiring Through Authenticity

First, let's clarify what leading with authenticity means. Being an Authentic Leader means being confident in oneself, leveraging one's unique innate strengths to inspire, influence, and lead others effectively. It involves a high level of self-awareness, self-regulation, psychological capital, and agency (each of which is discussed in detail with strategies and application tips in the following chapters).

When you lead with authenticity, everything you think, say, and do aligns with your values. You are genuine, resilient, and purpose-driven in both your personal and professional lives.

Humans have developed a desire for higher levels of meaning and impact beyond themselves. If you are reading this book, you are one of these amazing humans, wanting to find a better way to engage with your people, to inspire them, and create a greater impact in the world.

Why Did We Write This Book?

We wrote this book for three reasons:

1. **To redefine what powerful leadership looks and feels like.**
   For too long, leadership has been shaped by outdated models built on hierarchy, control, and conformity. We wrote this to challenge those norms, and to show that authenticity, compassion, and self-awareness are not "soft skills," but the true foundations of high performance.

2. **To give you practical tools that actually work in the real world.**
   After working with thousands of leaders across industries, countries, and cultures, we know that leadership theory alone isn't enough. You'll find evidence-based strategies, neuroscience, and lived experience distilled into simple, actionable steps you can apply immediately, whether you're leading a team, a business, or yourself.

3. **To ignite a global shift toward courageous, Authentic Leadership.**

    Our mission is to create workplaces and communities where people feel seen, valued, and empowered to be their authentic selves. When leaders lead from authenticity, they don't just achieve better results, they create ripples of trust, wellbeing, and performance that change lives.

We know that traditional one-size-fits-all leadership models *do not work* in today's world. They create silos, indecision, internal conflict, and a lack of trust in a team. If you want strategies based on traditional leadership and change management, then this book is not for you.

We've gone beyond traditional tactics, and know that when you show up as your authentic self and understand what this means and how to achieve it, you will have more energy, make decisions with more ease, and have a greater and more sustainable impact on your team. In turn, your team will have a safe space to admit and learn from mistakes, be more productive, and experience more cohesion, fun, and innovation throughout their day.

Ultimately, Authentic Leadership creates opportunities to fully embrace your true self and creates greater impact, influence and revenue, for you and your organization.

Who Are We To Write This Book?

We are Dr Elizabeth Pritchard and Christine Burns, Co-founders of WALT Institute, where we help people bust through self-doubt, cultivate a champions' mindset, and lead with courage, clarity, and confidence.

Between us, we bring over five decades of experience inspiring leaders across business, education, and elite sports. We have seen firsthand what ignites peak performance, accelerates growth and drives transformation, as well as what holds leaders back from reaching the next level.

Elizabeth brings a deep background in neuroscience, education, and leadership coaching, turning evidence into practical strategies that actually work in the real world.

Christine, CEO of WALT Institute, is a former elite athlete, an author, and performance coach who knows what it takes to build grit, resilience, and high-performing teams that win on and off the field.

Together, we have coached thousands of leaders and athletes, across organizations around the globe, helping them to step into their power and lead with authenticity. We have lived it, tested it, and proven it. Authentic Leadership isn't just what we teach, it 's who we are, how we live, and the legacy we are creating.

This Is Where It Gets Real

This is the power of the strategies we have in this book for you. A playbook that is evidence-based, is easy to understand, fun to implement, and has huge benefits for you and every person you lead. You get to choose to put these tiny tweaks into action and experience the joy and ease of leading authentically.

Get ready to uncover the transformative power of authenticity in simple, bite-sized strategies that you can implement today! Embrace Authentic Leadership to unlock your full potential and inspire those around you to a much higher level of performance.

Let's dive in and explore the extraordinary power of authenticity together.

Section One: BEing

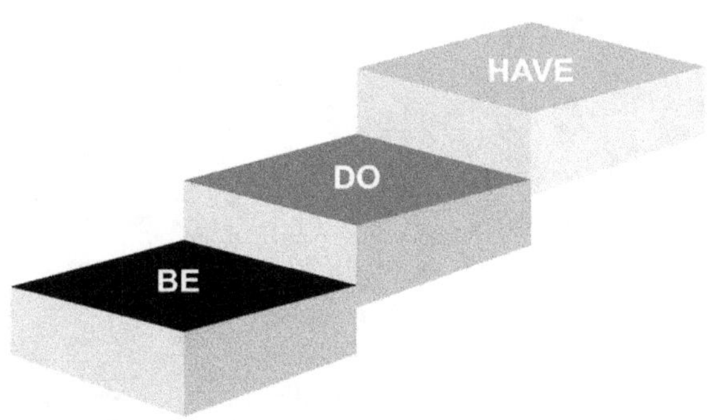

Who Are You Showing Up As?

BEing is the foundation of Authentic Leadership. It starts with the courage to look inward, cultivate self-awareness, and show up with intention. This means being grounded in your values, knowing your purpose, and regulating your thoughts, emotions, and actions with integrity. Authentic Leadership emphasizes the power of conscious choice, choosing how to respond rather than react, and choosing who to be in every situation.

In this section, we explore what it truly means to BE an Authentic Leader - what it looks like, sounds like, and feels like in practice. You'll discover how to build this way of being into your daily habits, so it becomes who you are, not just what you do. When you shift who you are BEing, everything else transforms - your actions, your impact, and ultimately, your results.

CHAPTER 1

BEing Self Aware: Stepping Into Your Self-Awareness

"You can carve your own path, be your own kind of leader. We need to create a new generation of leadership that is empathetic and strong."
—*Jacinda Ardern (Former Prime Minister of Aotearoa, New Zealand)*

Elizabeth

The first time I stepped up to lead authentically, it did not go well. I was a new graduate in a team of health professionals. I was overconfident, I knew the treatment plans we were discussing, I knew that I was *right* and they were *wrong*, and I knew what was best for my client.

I alienated some people, created awkwardness within the team, and had to rebuild some relationships, and credibility along the way, before I regained respect.

As I look back on this interaction, I now see through my experience as an Authentic Leader that this was not confidence, but rather ego and arrogance. I believed I was right, and therefore everyone else was wrong. I mistakenly thought there was only one way to see the situation and what needed to occur, and that I had every right to be angry and frustrated with their lack of knowledge.

You might see yourself in this scenario, or you might not, but when we develop self-awareness and self-regulation, we realize that there is no *right and wrong*. We realize that there are just differences in perspective. When we lead authentically, we understand that no *one* person has to win or make the other party a *loser.*

Instead, we get to notice our thoughts and responses, choose our *state* (our *current internal condition*; the blend of our physiology, thoughts, emotions, focus, and energy in any given moment), choose the meaning we give to any situation or interaction, and then decide to listen openly (or not).

When we lead authentically, we create the skill of noticing, pausing, and then choosing our response.

The Challenge Of Being A Newcomer

Fast forward about three decades from this experience, where I walk into a totally new team and a newly created role. The team is very close and has worked together for two years or more. They work hard and even hang out together. They are tight, committed, vibrant, and excel at what they do.

Walking into a team like this can go one of two ways:

1. You always feel like an outsider, or
2. You quickly develop rapport, and find a place within the team that is uniquely yours.

I followed the principles that Christine and I teach in this book to develop my skills for leading authentically.

I set myself up for success each day before I walk in the door or go online. I learn to be myself in every situation with confidence and certainty, am open and vulnerable, lead with transparency, converse with candor and compassion, and fit into the team fast. I know who I am, I don't have anything to prove, I don't have to win, and I do not seek approval from others.

I openly and honestly listen, be myself in every interaction, weigh ideas, and observe people without judging or jumping to conclusions. I find their strengths, celebrate these with them, and boost the team dynamics and outputs. I go into every situation and conversation being *me*. Unapologetically me. I show up in alignment with my values and non-negotiables, with honesty, vibrancy, and a huge sense of fun.

Although this journey began in the past, I choose to tell it in the present tense, because this is how I live and lead today. The principles are no longer just lessons learned; they are the way I show up every single day.

What an incredible difference it makes.

I get to be *me*, and show up as my true authentic self in every situation, with every person in the team. This creates ease and flow for me and the team every day. I am not *trying* to please other people or be someone they will like. I am not waiting to receive approval or external validation for my actions or who I am. I am not allowing my unconscious patterns and limiting beliefs to rule my thoughts, behaviors and actions.

What I am doing is noticing and mastering my thoughts, allowing the space to choose my responses, standing in my self-belief, and treating every single person with genuine compassion and respect. I am a totally different person from that previous new grad of my past. I am an Authentic Leader who has learned about her true self, and has the skills to step into BEing her true authentic self, every step of the way.

Authentic Leadership And YOU

Some of you think that Authentic Leadership is about doing your own thing no matter what. That might include dressing however you want, saying whatever you want, following through only when it suits you, or ignoring others and even alienating people along the way. This is not Authentic Leadership. This is self-centered leading.

It's time to stop being in it for *me*, and start being in it for *we* and *us*.

Authentic leadership is about carving your own path, embracing vulnerability and strength, aligning your actions with your values, and fostering an environment where individuals can thrive as their true selves because *you* are showing up consistently with these values.

Before we can BE an Authentic Leader, we need to KNOW what we are aiming for. There are four specific components of Authentic Leadership that are vital for us to understand and take action on:

#1 **Self-awareness**: This is the foundation of Authentic Leadership. It involves understanding your strengths, challenges, values, and motivations. Understanding your triggers, beliefs, patterns, responses, and behaviors. By becoming more self-aware, you can lead with greater clarity and purpose.

#2 **Self-regulation:** This is about managing your emotions and behaviors in a way that aligns with your values and goals. It is about consciously, purposefully, and intentionally dialing things up and down, depending on the situation. It enables you to stay focused, resilient, and adaptable in the face of challenges and opportunities.

#3 **Psychological capital:** Encompasses the positive psychological resources that contribute to your success as a leader. This includes hope, efficacy, resilience, and optimism. Cultivating psychological capital will empower you to inspire and motivate others (see chapter 3 for more on this).

#4 **Agency:** This refers to your ability to take action and make decisions that align with your authentic self and follow through no matter what. You have mastered the Toxic Ten (see chapter 4) and don't allow yourself, other people, environments, past experiences, mindset, or contexts to stop you! Agency means having the confidence, courage, and certainty to lead with integrity and influence others positively.

Each of these components can be explored and developed on its own. When they are implemented and integrated with mastery, you create the unshakeable foundation of BEing an Authentic Leader.

The first two components (self-awareness and self-regulation) are inextricably intertwined, and when you expand your mastery in both areas, you allow honesty and transparency to arise. Some people identify these components as emotional intelligence; however, what we often find when working with leaders is that as soon as *emotions* come into play, people tend to get defensive, scared, or judge others as being *too emotional.*

They are often fearful that they will *lose control*, either of themselves or others. For this reason, we are going to use the separate terms of self-awareness and self-regulation, as they begin with SELF.

This is where Authentic Leadership always needs to start!

Self-Awareness

Self-awareness can be tricky to develop, as, unfortunately, we often have an inflated sense of how aware we are. According to research from Dr. Tasha Eurich (an Organizational Psychologist), nearly everyone believes they have self-awareness. However, statistics show that only around 10-15% of leaders actually are self-aware[1]. In fact, most of the people who profess that they are very self-aware, are actually the least aware.

Let's make sure you are in that 10-15% group.

Self-awareness incorporates noticing what is happening for yourself first. This is when you get to ask:

- *What am I thinking about in this moment?*
- *What are my beliefs about myself or the other person in this moment?*
- *What are my responses to other people and external situations?*

Self-awareness is the skill and ability to reflect on what is actually happening in the moment, and not just what we think is happening, which is clouded through our own isomorphs and tinted lenses. Once we notice what is going on, we can then consciously pause, come back to being present in the moment, and not run on automatic patterns that may not serve us. Then we can choose the next move we make, starting with our thoughts.

---

[1] Eurich T. *Insight: The surprising truth about how others see us, how we see ourselves, and why the answers matter more than we think.* New York: Crown Business; 2017.

Now, let's talk about our *Three-step NPC Formula* for growing your self-awareness.

The Three-Step NPC Formula:

Step one: Notice

Noticing is about recognizing what we are thinking, feeling, and doing, without attributing any blame, shame, guilt, or judgement to it. There are three ways we can hook into noticing:

- Through our thoughts and words
- Through our emotions and feelings within our bodies
- Through our actions and behaviors

We all have a natural bent for which one we hook into first, and once we recognize this in ourselves, we can begin to regulate what comes next.

Practice noticing the thoughts in your head at any specific time of the day. We have between 60,000 and 70,000 thoughts a day, and 90% of them are repeated from yesterday, the day before that, and so on.

Practice hooking into how you are feeling at specific times of the day, or set yourself a timer to notice what you are doing at regular intervals. When you set your timer to alert you two times a day for five days each week, you'll hear the stimulus (a great and unique sound/tune alert) and then you get to ask yourself: *What am I thinking in this moment / What am I feeling right now / What am I doing in this moment?*

By strengthening your skill of noticing, you will quickly recognize all three elements. With continued practice and mastery, you'll be able to identify the thought that sparked the feeling and triggered the action (more on this vital skill later). Consistently tuning into whatever you notice first then allows you to move seamlessly into step two.

Step two: Pause

Yes, it's that *simple*, but that doesn't mean it's *easy*.

Pausing means to stop, take a breath, and consciously choose to be in the moment. It means not thinking about the future of what needs to happen next, or worrying about something that happened in the past.

A pause can be 10 seconds, five minutes, or anything in between. That is enough time for you to put a pause between *noticing* and choosing your *next step*. When you are in a pause, you get to set yourself up to shift into a different state of mind, allowing yourself to *BE* in a different state.

Then, you instigate step three.

Step three: Choose Again

Step three is where you get to *choose* what comes next: What you are thinking, how you are feeling, and what action you will take. You get to choose to respond or not, to speak or not, to move or not.

You are choosing this intentionally, consciously, purposefully, and powerfully because you have put the pause in place. You have hit the *circuit breaker* button and stopped the spiral of thoughts, emotions, and automatic actions. You have stopped 'reacting' and are now *being purposeful* in everything you say and do. Your decisions are no longer coming from an automatic pattern or response.

Now that you have put steps 1 and 2 in place, there is a space where you get to choose! It can be a change in breathing, a shift in mental focus, choosing a different language (see chapter 5 on Supercharging your Language), dialing up or down an emotion, or a totally different action.

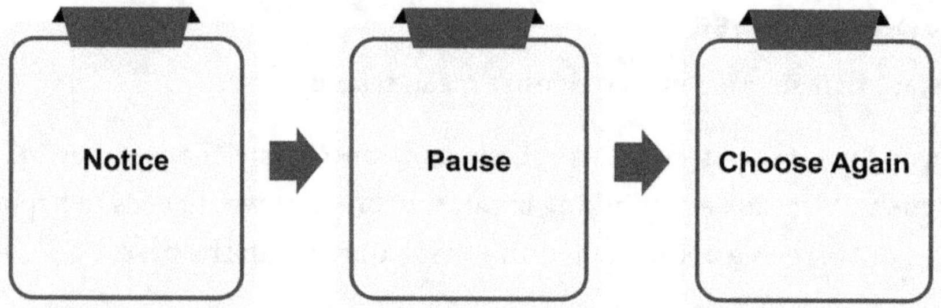

Figure 1: Three-Step NPC Formula – Grow Your Self-Awareness

Instigating the **Three-Step NPC Self-Awareness Formula** interrupts automatic response patterns and allows you to increase your self-awareness, choose a different response, and therefore, have a different outcome.

This may sound tricky to begin with, but remember, everything we share in this book *is doable*. We have taught thousands of leaders to do this, and you can do it too! You *can* instigate this strategy straight away. Then you get to practice it consistently until you have formed the new habit of elevating your self-awareness to the next level.

You get to choose to be one of the 10-15% of leaders who are self-aware!

Sam's Story

Take Sam for example. He loved his job as a leader of eight other people in his corporate team. He wanted the absolute best for each of them.

However, he realized that he was doing all the talking. His team often felt unclear about what needed to happen, and unrealistic demands from upper management frequently landed on Sam's shoulders within the confusion.

In response to these team issues, Sam began practicing our three-step method.

First, he noticed that when he was speaking without stopping, he tended to run out of breath. Next, he practiced recognizing this pattern and then purposefully began taking a pause. For Sam, this meant shifting his position and posture (either leaning forward or back in the chair, or when standing, shifting the weight from one leg to the other) and taking a deep breath in. Next, he practiced being comfortable with the pause so that he could allow space for others to respond.

He then learned to *choose again* in this pause, and purposefully chose the next step to instigate. Sometimes this was to ask a question of the team and then allow time for responses. Sometimes it was to check in with specific people in meetings and ask them to rephrase their understanding of what he was saying.

Over a period of three weeks, Sam found that he was being listened to more, that management was trusting him more, and that the team was beginning to find greater areas of working together with clarity and higher levels of productivity. He even found that he was not being *dumped on* by upper management as much anymore, and that they were beginning to show more trust.

You can do this too. It all starts with being self-aware. Aware of yourself without any blame, shame, guilt, or judgment. Without beating yourself up for *doing that thing again*. This means accepting yourself in the moment and knowing that you may react, get ruffled, lose your cool, overtalk, or withdraw. These are just patterns that we learn in life, and because we have learned them over time, we can also learn *different patterns* that serve us better.

You get to choose to change these patterns with awareness. It's about learning how not to jump into the automatic patterns of reacting. It's about not continuing to repeat the patterns you have created that no longer serve you, and purposefully, consciously, intentionally, and powerfully creating new patterns with self-awareness and self-regulation.

Noticing The Triggers

When people start mastering the skill of noticing, they often recognize they are using the word *triggered*. They often say, "That triggered me," or "I can't do that, it's triggering." This language can become a type of excuse to explain our responses when we feel upset, overwhelmed, or react outside of being our best.

Constantly retelling the same stories and reliving old experiences keeps us stuck, producing repeated outcomes such as anxiety, depression, frustration, anger, guilt, or resentment.

When we cling to something that happened in the past, where we continually talk about it and refer to it, replaying the event again and again like a never-ending replay of a movie, we *feel* the emotions of the *trauma* again and again. By repeatedly retelling these stories, we are *choosing* to stay in the pain of the past, and this prevents us from stepping up or moving forward.

Remember: There's no blame, no shame, no guilt, and no judgment of self when this happens. This pattern is simply a clever protection mechanism that you developed in order to keep yourself safe.

However, since you have this book in your hands, it's clear that you have decided this is no longer where you want to be. You no longer want to be stuck in the pain of past experiences, and no longer want to hold yourself back from becoming your best self. Go you!

These Authentic Leadership strategies will absolutely help you to break these old patterns and create different ones going forward. Whether your *triggering* stories are work-related situations or things that have happened in your personal life, these strategies work. Being *triggered* is common. However, you can train yourself to have a more empowering response whenever those thoughts and emotions show up again.

How To Implement This Strategy

When you notice something is triggering, think: ***A trigger is an invitation to explore.*** Nothing has meaning except the meaning you give it, and this *trigger* is an opportunity for you to explore the reaction you are having. Recognize the thoughts and the emotions that show up.

Call it like it is, call it *as is*. Be true to yourself and the reaction you are having, and then, choose a different response. An amazing quote in Jefferson Fisher's book is: "What triggers you, teaches you - *if* you're willing to learn".[2]

After noticing something powerful has stirred within us, we get to choose. Choose the meaning we give the event, choose our feelings around the event, and choose how we respond to it. Even when old patterns rise, we are not bound by them. By observing our reactions, we gain the power to choose how we think, feel, and respond, which creates a new path forward.

If we stay stuck in the event, replaying it over and over again in our minds, and talk about it constantly, it becomes our identity. It becomes who we BE. It begins to define us, what we think, what we feel, how we respond, and what we have. It then determines what we can and cannot do.

When we notice our response to the person or event, we can then choose again - choose our thoughts, our emotions, and our actions going forward.

This, of course, does not excuse the other person for their action or inaction. It's also not about pretending that everything is peachy or that the event didn't happen at all. This is not about ignoring real challenges or allowing others to walk all over us, hurt us, or other people.

This *is* about taking back your personal control of what you *can* control. It is about owning your response and choosing again. Choosing to release our grip on the trauma, choosing to release the emotions that no longer serve us, choosing to release our negative responses, and choosing not to be controlled by the event that happened.

If you have been triggered by something recently, take a moment to pause and reflect. Remember, this moment is an invitation to explore. *Emotions*

---

[2] Fisher J. *The Next Conversation: Argue Less, Talk More.* London: Penguin General UK; 2025. (p90)

do not hurt us, they are just feedback. A signal that indicates we are responding to a stimulus, and our response is within our control.

We simply get to practice the NPC method.

Another tool that helps you explore your response is asking really amazing questions. Questions ARE the answer! When an event occurs, ask yourself these 5 questions and embrace your opportunity to explore with openness, curiosity, authenticity, and self-acceptance.

1. What is this reaction about?
2. What can I learn about myself in this moment?
3. What would it take for me to accept myself in this moment?
4. Who would I be without this reaction?
5. What different response could I choose right now?

You then get to *choose again*, to recognize what you DO have control over in this moment. These are *your* thoughts, *your* feelings, and *your* actions.

We know through research from Dr Joe Dispenza and many others that our thoughts release a chemical reaction, which we then interpret as feelings. So, if we change our thoughts, we change the feeling.[3] [4] Keep this in mind as you continue to read the strategies in this book.

As Michael Singer puts it, we are choosing to hold onto the event and stay in the suffering.[5]

This may sound harsh, but it's the truth. If you cling to the memory of when you didn't get a promotion, when someone passed you over for someone else, when a client said *no*, when a team member ignored your

---

[3] Dispenza J. *Breaking the habit of being yourself: How to lose your mind and create a new one.* Carlsbad (CA): Hay House; 2012.

[4] Lipton BH. T*he biology of belief: Unleashing the power of consciousness, matter & miracles.* 10th anniversary ed. Carlsbad (CA): Hay House; 2010.

[5] Singer MA. *The untethered soul: The journey beyond yourself.* Chicago: Turabian; 2013.

ideas, or when a manager passed off your ideas as their own, then you are choosing to stay a victim. Choosing to stay stuck in the *past.*

If you're ready to break free from limiting beliefs and patterns, keep reading. Our strategies can provide a proven path to help you release the grip of past trauma and step fully into your own truth.

This Can Work for You, Too

Hundreds of people have experienced real transformation through our Authentic Leadership strategies, even those who had spent years in therapy and identified limited progress. While we are not psychologists, in just a few coaching or training sessions with us, clients have reported remarkable shifts in self-control, confidence, and overall leadership presence.

Just last week, in our *first* coaching session, one client said: "Oh my God, I just had a breakthrough with that. I've been going to therapy for three years and you busted that apart in half a session". This change in mindset is powerful, if you choose to embrace the strategies and put them into action.

These strategies work. Consistently apply them, and you will see results.

When you master these components, you get to recognize and choose your response to any person, event, or situation you have experienced or find yourself in. This can include the labels of *triggers, trauma,* or *challenges* that crop up at any time. One of the most profound things we have found in our work when growing Authentic Leaders is that *the past does not define us,* and we get to choose our response to any and every event that has or does occur.

A Cautionary Tale Of Being And Choosing To Stay Triggered:

When working with leaders across all different organizations and countries, we often hear them talk about situations, events, or people who *trigger* them. Remember that if we keep retelling the same story of hurt or betrayal again and again, then this is what we focus on, and ultimately, who we will become.

Gemma's Story

Gemma faced a familiar problem: Despite her talents and commitment, she kept hitting invisible barriers in her personal and professional growth. She decided to choose a path of Authentic Leadership, determined to step fully into her own strength, self-awareness, and self-regulation.

In our work with Gemma, she embraced the principles of Authentic Leadership with great gusto. She committed to learning, practicing, and embedding the habits that would allow her to lead with clarity, confidence, and authenticity. Her efforts were paying off. She was doing well and beginning to experience levels of success she had never known before.

And then... she got scared. The higher she rose and grew, the more the unknown seemed to loom. Old patterns crept in. The Toxic Ten (Chapter 4) emerged. These are 10 common behaviors or mindsets that quietly undermine our effectiveness, and how we show up every day. In Gemma's case, these were manifesting as *self-sabotage* and *procrastination*.

At the heart of this pattern was one area of Gemma's life that she kept replaying and retelling: An incident from several years ago at work which she had labeled as *traumatic*. She had experienced psychological bullying from a manager, which had left her confidence shattered, her self-belief undermined, and her sense of control stripped away.

To Gemma, this moment became life-defining. She held onto it as part of her identity, seeing herself as a victim. Triggers, certain words, tones, or people would reactivate the story, causing her to retreat, procrastinate, and cling to familiarity for safety, even as she was making enormous strides in her leadership.

This *trauma* had become a self-reinforcing loop: The more she identified with it, the more it shaped her behavior, keeping her stuck in the same role and sabotaging the progress she was capable of.

During our coaching sessions together, Gemma began to realize that patterns are just that, patterns. They once kept her safe, but they didn't need to define who she became. With self-awareness, she began to pause, notice, and choose differently. She chose to consciously build new habits, repeat them, and let them become her default ways of showing up.

Gemma started to craft a new identity, with boundaries, intentional choices, energy, and allowing moments of joy. She chose who she allowed into her circle, recognized what and who drained her, and stepped away from it. Step by step, she was becoming the person she hadn't been before, the Authentic Leader she aspired to be.

By facing the fear, embracing the importance of practice, and breaking old patterns, Gemma was no longer defined by her past trauma. Instead, she was defined by the deliberate, consistent choices she made to BE authentic, *DO* in alignment, and ultimately *HAVE* the impact and influence she desired.

Keep Reading

You may be thinking about pausing here to argue with us. You might be saying: "But you don't know what he/she/they did to me," or "You don't know how traumatic it was for me."

One of the most-common experiences we have when working with people who are becoming Authentic Leaders is reminding them that we *all* have sticky things in our past that keep coming up for us.

None of those sticky moments are better or worse than anyone else's. We cannot compare these events. If we do, it's like seeking to gain a *badge of honor*, to win at having the biggest, worst, most horrific past event. This is another BS pattern we see in people, but remember, it's just a pattern.

This book will help you break those patterns and create new ones which serve you more.

Everything you have been through is part of the incredible, strong, and accomplished person you have become. Without these events and experiences, you wouldn't be who you are. And who you are is totally *AMAZING, MAGNIFICENT, and YOU freakin' ROCK!*

Elizabeth

I lived through sexual abuse at the age of eight. I used to constantly get stuck in the event, replaying it, being *triggered* by it. But by applying the strategies we teach in this book, I now view that past event as a gift of learning and growth, not as a constant trigger or trauma.

First, I call it *as is.* Yes, the perpetrator was 100% in the wrong. Yes, I was not at all to blame. Yes, he took control over me and in the most horrific way and I cannot change the event in any way.

BUT I get to choose what impact that past event has on me now.

The abuse that occurred is my invitation to identify the incredible tenacity, strength, and GRIT that I have developed.

GRIT as Angela Duckworth defines it, is the combination of *passion* and *perseverance* for long-term goals.[6] It's what keeps you moving when motivation fades and the path gets rocky. It's the fuel that turns discipline into devotion, effort into mastery, and setbacks into stepping stones.

Gritty leaders don't just survive challenges, they grow stronger because of them. They understand that success isn't built in grand gestures or lucky breaks. Success is forged in the daily grind, the micro-wins, and the relentless decision to keep showing up.

---

[6] Duckworth A. *Grit: The power of passion and perseverance.* New York: Scribner; 2016.

Recognizing and celebrating effort is also an important part of building GRIT.

Living with GRIT, is an invitation to learn how to let go of the past, let go of the hurt, guilt, resentment, blame, shame, anger, and anything else connected to the event. My strength and love of life that I exhibit every day, that I have trained myself in, *is not in spite* of the event, but *because of it.*

Christine

For me, a trigger of rejection occurred when I was at the top of my game as a New Zealand hockey player, but was passed over for the Olympic selection (not once but twice), because of the coach's selection bias. This was a time of intense disappointment and anger, all because of someone else's beliefs about the team, the number of years a player was expected to have in the game before being promoted, and the city/region the player was from.

This could have created bitterness, long-term anger, and even hatred, but in these moments, we all get to choose the meaning we give to these events and how we respond to them. You will see in chapter 6 how we go through the *Calling it as is* process of feeling the pain, validating your instant response, and choosing again.

You *can* learn to train yourself to step into your authenticity, use the NPC method, and choose a different response, going forward.

We can choose to see our past as difficult, tough, traumatic, *ruined my life* events, OR we can choose to see them as they are - an event that happened, an opportunity for us to choose the meaning we attribute to it, and an opportunity to choose again.

In situations like these, it is nearly impossible to leap straight from feeling a negative response to a positive one. Positive thinking fails in these moments because it denies the truth of what we are feeling. If we pretend that we are not hurting, we create inner conflict between our thoughts and our emotions.

Instead, the key is to first work through the experience using the techniques we've outlined. Once we shift from negative to neutral, we have noticed, paused, regained control, and are able to choose a different, more constructive action moving forward.

We have created meaning to interpret things as neutral. How powerful it is to go from triggers, trauma, negative, tough, and hard challenges to neutral! When you learn that every event can be seen as negative, neutral, or positive, then, with self-awareness and self-regulation, you get the opportunity to choose to view everything as neutral.

It is what it is, and you get to choose the meaning you give to it. This is a game changer!

It just takes conscious awareness (noticing), self-regulation (beginning with a pause), and a decision and action, to choose again.

What Is The Meaning We Choose?

"Nothing has meaning except the meaning we give it."
—*Linda Belzile Buisson*

This is a belief that has been drummed into us by our amazing coach, Linda. She leads with authenticity, calls things as they are, and consistently demonstrates the courage and skill to challenge, stretch our thinking, and elevate both how we show up individually and how we do our work. Through her guidance, we've grown in confidence, clarity and capability, transforming not just our approach, but the results we create.

Choosing the meaning is a vital choice that you can learn as a habit, which will catapult your Authentic Leadership practice to the next level. We get to choose the meaning we give to any situation and experience. We can choose to see things as big and huge and tough and difficult, or we can approach them as an opportunity.

If I choose to believe that another person is *always out to get me*, or *doing it to get back at me*, or that *no one ever supports me*, then I am setting myself up as a victim. If I choose to believe that *this person does things totally differently from me,* or *they are doing the best they can with what they've got,* or *I always have people around that help when I let them,* then I have different thoughts.

Choosing new thoughts creates different emotions, which leads to a different outcome.

It's my choice.

When I choose to remember that every situation is an opportunity and that life happens *for* me, not *to* me, I can learn from it and step into new ways of thinking, *DOing,* and *BEing.*

What If I Notice I Am Stuck?

Good work. You have done the first step - you noticed!

We cannot change if things are not in our awareness. *Awareness brings change.* If you are now becoming aware of the patterns of being stuck in the past - holding onto the trauma, reveling in the victim persona, repeating the same hurt, angry, or betrayed story to yourself or others - *you now get to* choose to release this.

As Michael Singer states, *"Suffering stems from resisting reality and clinging to preferences. When we let go of our attachments, we open ourselves to peace and freedom."* If we are not intentionally releasing these things from the past, then we are choosing to cling onto them, and therefore choosing to stay in the suffering.[7]

Ouch - That one landed! This is what I used to do all the time: Hold on to the bad stuff or cling to the resentment, the pain, and the judgment. Not anymore.

---

[7] Singer MA. *The Untethered Soul: The Journey Beyond Yourself.* Oakland (CA): New Harbinger Publications; 2007.

Next, I'll share a valuable tool with you to help you get past these old habits. I have recorded a meditative imagery activity for you to go through, to provide you with a way to release yourself from holding on and clinging to suffering.

Access your Cord-Cutting meditation HERE:
https://waltinstitute.com/cordcuttingmeditation

Cutting the ties of the emotional hold these events have on you allows you to release these emotions, stop past patterns, bring the meaning of the event into neutral, and step into your authenticity. Step into a place where you can lead from the *now*.

Become the future Authentic Leader that you are destined to be! Mastering the art of self-awareness and self-regulation is so powerful for individuals and teams, and it is a must to start with YOU.

Start with noticing, pausing, and choosing again. Choose to reframe the event, choose the meaning you give to whatever occurs each day. Choose to shift into a neutral perspective. Then you will identify the opportunities and moments of learning and begin to lead yourself and others with authenticity.

Chapter Takeaways:

BEing **before** *DOing* - Authentic Leadership begins with who you are *BEing*, not what you are *DOing*. Your actions reflect your inner state.

Authentic Leadership is built on four core components:

- *Self-awareness* – knowing yourself
- *Self-regulation* – managing yourself
- *Psychological capital* – building hope, efficacy, resilience, and optimism
- *Agency* – taking values-aligned action

Authentic Leadership Starts with *Me* - and then become *we.*

NPC Formula – Use *Notice, Pause, Choose Again* to shift automatic patterns and increase your self-awareness to choose a better response.

Triggers are Opportunities – Triggers are an invitation to explore.

Emotions are Feedback – Emotions do not hurt you, they are simply feedback.

Creating my own reality - Life happens *for* me, not *to* me.

Meaning-Making – Nothing has any meaning except the meaning you give it; choose interpretations that empower rather than limit you.

Rewrite the Story – Stories are all just made up stuff anyway, so make up a good story. Growth happens when you stop repeating old stories and consciously create a new narrative.

The Past Does Not Define You - Your current decisions, focus, and habits do.

Shift to a Neutral Perspective – When emotions run high, move from negative to neutral first.

Exploring Your Responses – Questions *are* the answer: What can I learn about myself?

CHAPTER 2

Being On An Even Keel: The Authentic Leader's Path To Self-Regulation

"You have power over your mind - not outside events.
Realize this, and you will find strength."
—*Marcus Aurelius*

Christine

There were two minutes left on the clock. We were up 2–1 in the final of the New Zealand National Hockey Tournament. The stadium was thumping, with roars from the crowd and teammates shouting; adrenaline was high. I was playing goalie for our Manawatu Women's 'A' Team.

This was our first National Final, and the stakes couldn't have been higher.

Every breath inside my helmet felt tight. My heartbeat pounded louder than the chants in the crowd.

Pressure? Absolutely. It was a defining moment.

Then, a pause in play. Our captain sprinted towards me, locked eyes, and calmly said, "Stay focused in this moment right now. Be here now."

It was like the world slowed. Clarity returned. A calm confidence surged. My shoulders relaxed.

I was back in control - not just of my position on the turf, but of my entire internal state. I called the defense into position with precision. I could anticipate the opposition's next move like I had a sixth sense.

A sharp shot came in. I was already there. Stop. Clear. The ball was well upfield, and then the final whistle blew.

We were National Champions.

That moment was not luck. It was not talent. It was self-regulation in action-anchoring my mindset in the perceived chaos and finding rhythm in the storm. It's the shift from overwhelm and reaction to refined focus and precise action. This sort of technique can apply to every person, in every situation.

Why Self-Regulation Is The Authentic Leadership Edge

As the leader of our defense, I didn't just protect the goal, I stabilized the team. When I stayed steady, they stayed steady. When I called with clarity and certainty, it created a ripple of composure across the field.

In elite performance, this level of stability is not optional; it's essential. Within Authentic Leadership, this ability is even more important.

We've all worked with those unpredictable leaders. One day, they're Eeyore, dragging their feet and being pessimistic, always finding the negative side of everything, and next, they're like a purple minion, losing all self-control and in full emotional meltdown. Or worse, they rely on over-the-top fake positives, like Olaf the snowman who dreams of living in a continuous summer.

Are you like one of these cartoon characters, allowing your identity to be defined by your patterns and external people? Are you without self-awareness or self-regulation?

Or are you consciously riding your own rhythm, with an even keel?

Authentic Leaders don't do emotional whiplash. They don't show up in a negative space and stay there. They don't explode and take their frustrations out on the team, and they don't put their head in the sand pretending everything is okay.

They notice. They regulate. They ride the rhythm. They know and understand that their emotional energy has an impact on all of the people they are around, and they use it consciously, purposefully, and intentionally.

The Ship In The Storm

Martin Seligman, the founder of Positive Psychology, uses a metaphor that I believe identifies the concept we must all embrace to be a successful Authentic Leader. He talks about being like a ship on an "even keel." In rough seas, an unbalanced ship will tip, drift, or capsize. But a ship on an even keel weathers the storm and stays the course.

As an Authentic Leader in any organization, storms are frequent with varying sizes and, at times, persistently unforgiving: pressure, deadlines, relationships, metrics, people challenges, and curveballs.

The question is, can you stay upright, focused, and composed? Seligman teaches that self-regulation is not about suppressing emotions, it's about emotional agility. Being able to notice, name, and navigate your emotions so they *serve you* rather than sabotage you.[8]

Let me share something very important with you here: The person in the room with the broadest, most conscious emotional range has the most influence.

This means that when you are able to notice what you are feeling inside, have a broad range of emotions and intensity, then you are able to exhibit a wide range of responses. When you have a broad range of emotions, you can then choose your response with more breadth, are more able to dial-up and dial-down these emotions, and can provide the modeling to your team in doing so.

---

[8] Seligman MEP. *Flourish: A visionary new understanding of happiness and well-being.* New York: Free Press; 2011.

This is how you lead without force. This is how you create psychological safety. This is how you build elite teams.

Let's get a bit tactical here, because theory without tools is just useless noise. Here are three strategies I use personally and coach high-performers to master:

1. The Mindfulness Power Move

What to do:

Develop a micro mindfulness practice - something small, consistent, and real.

I often ask clients: "Do you drink coffee?" (Or tea, or matcha. Whatever works for you.)

You can turn that *coffee moment* into a daily ritual for grounding your nervous system. You can do this whether you purchase that liquid gold at the Café, make it yourself with a machine, or just a good old instant drink.

Here's what you can practice with consistency:

- When you start the process of making your drink, engage all your senses.
- Listen to the machine, the bubbles, the grinder.
- Smell the aroma as it fills the room.
- Watch the colours change as the liquid pours.
- Feel the cup in your hands.
- Take a sniff as you bring that vessel up to your mouth.
- Taste that first sip like it's the very first time. Hold it. Savor it.

That's your *coffee moment* or also known as *active mindfulness*. Let's *choose* to do this five out of seven days, not because we're lazy, but because we reject perfectionism. When we set targets that we CAN achieve, we get a dopamine rush of success, and this trains our brain to seek this more and do this more.

We set ourselves up for success and celebrate our amazing achievements.

Remember, *consistency beats intensity*. When you repeat these methods with consistency, this moment becomes automatic. Then, you can add two to three deep, focused breaths to enhance being present in the moment.

Notice your breath. Then your body. Then your emotions.

Why does this practice work?

Mindfulness activities strengthen your prefrontal cortex, which is like the *CEO* of your brain. It reduces stress by decreasing the production of stress hormones, which in turn reduces inflammation in the body.

Mindfulness has also been shown to lengthen our *telomeres* in the brain (these are protective caps at the ends of our chromosomes, which can support a longer life and reduce age-related diseases). Mindfulness allows you to respond rather than react and is the secret weapon for staying calm under fire.

2. Build A Strategic Support Crew

What to put in place:

Curate a crew of three to five people who have your back mentally, emotionally, physically, and spiritually. These people are not just your cheerleaders, but are your challengers and co-elevators. The ones who lift you, stretch you, and hold you accountable.

Identify who you have in your crew. Start by:

- Mapping your current network. Where are the gaps, the soft spots? Those who support, no matter what?
- Schedule consistent check-ins with your crew.
- Be explicit about the support you need from them. (This may be different for each person.)

- Offer value in return. Support flows both ways! What is the level of reciprocity that you offer as well as receive?

Why it works:

Research clearly describes that Authentic Leaders with strong, trusted support systems have higher levels of resilience and perform more consistently. Humans are made for social connection.[9] We all need anchors and support. Get yours in place.

3. Create Rhythmic Levels Of Energy

Let's move beyond the old *work–life balance* cliché.

Balance implies equal weight on both sides, and that's simply not how life works. If we tried to keep *work* and *life* in perfect balance, we'd need the same intensity, pressure, and energy in both. That would only double the load and drive us faster towards burnout.

Instead, what if we focused on *integration*; intentionally designing how we show up, where we put our attention, and how we recharge? When we align our values, purpose, and energy across all areas of life, we don't need to *balance* anything. We create *flow*.

So Let's Think About Things We Do Every Day As A Rhythm

What you need is an energy *rhythm* - a way of pushing *and* pulling. A method of easing up *and* flowing forward. A way of finding the rhythm in your life when sometimes some things are more acute, and others are ebbing away like an orchestral symphony. Sometimes it's full of noise and percussion and all instruments playing fortissimo, and other times there are one or two instruments lyrically playing a single pianissimo melody.

---

[9] Katzenbach JR, Smith DK. *The wisdom of teams: Creating the high-performance organization.* Boston (MA): Harvard Business School Press; 1993.

Authentic Leaders don't chase balance, they cultivate alignment and rhythm.

What's required to ride your rhythm?

Here are some suggestions:

- Morning: 10–20 mins of movement before screens.
- Midday: Device-free 10-minute walk after lunch.
- Between tasks: A 30-second pause to breathe, reflect, and reset.
- Evening: Tech-free time with people who matter.
- Weekly: 60-minute check-in with yourself; journal, reflect, recalibrate.

Why it works:

Elite athletes and elite leaders share one secret: They manage energy, not just time. You need cycles of performance and renewal. Otherwise, you'll lose your edge and so will your team.

How I set myself up every morning:

- Smile upon waking and recognize something amazing about myself.
- Choose what my intention is for the day and how I'm going to show up throughout.
- Take an ice bath dip (five out of seven days), accompanied by some breathing exercises.
- Do a workout, take a walk, or have one movement session.

Then I look at what's on for the day and set myself up with good, energy-producing nutrition and always have fun in my day.

Fun is my number one value. It's not an afterthought or something I squeeze in between serious moments, it's how I live. Fun fuels creativity, strengthens resilience, and connects people on a human level. Neuroscience shows us that when we experience joy and laughter, our brains release dopamine and endorphins.

These are the powerful chemicals that boost energy, learning, and performance. For me, fun is a lifestyle, not a luxury. It's how I stay energized, authentic, and fully engaged with life and the people around me.

When we lead with fun, we don't just work better, we live better.

Mindful Leadership In Action

James, a senior leader in financial services, was heading into a career-defining regulatory investigation. This is when the financial authorities examine every detail of how the organization operates, such as the systems, decisions, and leadership actions. Nothing goes unnoticed.

This is one of those moments that can make or break a leader.

Previously, pressure like this would have caused him to spin out, attempt to control everything, micromanaging, and burning out his team. But this time was different. He had a daily ritual, his coffee moment. From the first sound of the grinder to his first sip, James unleashed all his senses and focused on complete attention to be in the moment. It grounded him.

He added in short mindful pauses throughout the day. He paused before and after meetings. He checked in with his mind and body before tough decisions and having courageous conversations.

He didn't go it alone. He met weekly with me, his mindset coach, someone who gave him an honest, high-level perspective, who would ask the questions that would shift him to new heights, and who would hold him accountable. I was the person who would tell him what he needed to hear, not just what he wanted to hear.

The result? James was well and truly in command of his ship. He embraced the rhythm of his life each day. His team felt supported, communication stayed open, and they navigated the investigation better than their competitors. James didn't just survive the storm. He led through it. That's the power of self-regulation.

Your Turn To Lead – From Chaos To Clarity

You don't need to be an international athlete or a CEO to apply these techniques. You need to care enough about your Authentic Leadership to make small, daily, purposeful, tiny tweaks. When you instigate these strategies to set yourself up each day, you will find that you are being more present, more able to come back to neutral, and better able to connect with and lead your team.

The effect of this is more highly motivated team members, higher levels of productivity, stronger mental health throughout, and ultimately, higher levels of revenue for yourself and your organization.

Here's where to begin:

1. **Choose one mindfulness ritual** - even if it's just your morning *coffee moment.*
2. **Reach out to *one* person** today to begin strengthening your support network.
3. **Create *one* micro energy ritual** in your day - maybe it's a breath pause between tasks or a phone-free dinner.

Anchor these strategies into your life, and you will feel the shift. Emotional regulation isn't a distant ideal; it's a practiced rhythm, and when you ride the rhythm, others will too.

Final Thought:

The world needs more leaders who are steady in the storm. Not robotic, not emotionless, but emotionally aware, grounded, and strong. Be that leader. Be the calm in the chaos. Be on an even keel, and then step back and watch how others rise with you.

Chapter Takeaways:

Self-Regulation as a Superpower – Leadership excellence starts with mastering your internal state, not suppressing it. Calm is your competitive advantage.

Energy Sets the Tone – Your presence influences others; when you're steady and grounded, your team feels it too.

Ride the Rhythm – Authentic Leaders stay present and responsive rather than reactive. They don't have high highs, or low lows, and are on an even keel.

Emotional Range Equals Influence – The person with the broadest emotional range, has the most influence and impact in the room.

Micro-Moments Matter – Short mindful moments reset your nervous system, reduce stress, and enhance performance.

The Coffee Moment – Engage all of your five senses in that moment; a simple act of being present.

Consistency Over Intensity – Is not about perfection or giving 100% all the time; it's about showing up as your true self, in that moment with consistency.

Fun Fuels Focus – Have Fun. You get the quickest release of happy chemicals to set you up for creativity, learning, and resilience.

You Are the Captain of Your Ship – In times of challenge, your steadiness provides safety and direction for those you lead.

Build Your Crew – Leadership is not a solo act. Surround yourself with people who challenge, support, and stretch you.

Manage Your Energy – Sustainable performance comes from choosing your state, honing your focus, and aligning your energy with your purpose.

Mindfulness in Action – Awareness of thoughts and emotions allows you to respond with precision, not impulse.

Be the Calm in the Chaos – The world doesn't need more frantic leaders; it needs grounded ones who inspire stability and confidence.

Leading Forward:

What's your one key takeaway from the chapter (of course there will be more), that you are going to take action on NOW?

CHAPTER 3

Authentic Leadership And How We Do It

"Authentic Leadership isn't about what you learn or DO, it's about who you BE every single moment of every day"
—WALT Institute

In this chapter, we invite you into a raw and honest conversation about what Authentic Leadership truly means to us.

Authentic Leadership is not a scripted checklist, a set of rules for performance, or a textbook model. It is not a one-size-fits-all formula. It's personal. It's lived, and it looks different for each of us, while still leading to the same powerful place: Living and leading from who we truly are.

Authentic Leadership is about *who we are* BEing (as individuals and leaders), how we choose to show up in the world, and how we walk alongside others with courage, compassion, and integrity.

That's why, in this chapter, you will hear from both of us as we answer four pivotal questions that have shaped our leadership journeys in unique yet deeply aligned ways.

Our perspectives are different, yet our commitment is the same: To embody Authentic Leadership in every moment. Even when it's hard, uncertain, or messy. You'll read our honest reflections, the lessons we didn't see coming, and the raw moments that nearly broke us - but ultimately made us stronger. We'll share candid stories, be vulnerable, unfiltered, and offer our hard-won wisdom. These are the lessons that shaped us, so you can accelerate your own leadership growth without making the same missteps.

As you move through this chapter, we invite you not just to listen, but to reflect. If you are still holding back and doubting that Authentic Leadership is right for you, consider this your invitation behind the scenes: To see the real us, to reflect on your own path, and to take bold, aligned action towards greatness in your leadership.

What do these questions stir in *you?*

Now, let's dive in.

What Does Authentic Leadership Mean To You, And How Has This Evolved Over Time?

Understanding Authentic Leadership

Elizabeth

Authentic Leadership, to me, means being so deeply in tune with who you are that this *knowing* becomes your internal compass, guiding every action, reaction, and interaction. It's about being self-led. Not seeking validation or approval from the external world, but having the courage to stand in your truth, even when it's uncomfortable or unpopular.

When you lead authentically, you're driven from the inside out. You've cultivated the ability to pause, reflect, and respond, rather than react. This self-regulation is what separates Authentic Leaders from reactive ones. It's not about being perfect. It's about being aware enough to choose your response with intention, grace, and alignment.

I know I'm BEing authentic when I feel grounded. When I've paused long enough to check in with myself, not just intellectually, but emotionally as well. I'm no longer caught up in stories like *What will they think of me?* or *Maybe I should do this, because…*

I am learning to have the courage to be disliked, which paradoxically often makes me more respected and trusted. This is because I'm not desperately seeking approval or reinforcement from others, because I've found validation within myself first.

When I'm being authentic, I make decisions from a place of clarity and alignment with my values. I'm not driven by ego, fear, or the need to please. I'm simply being me.

It Wasn't Always This Way

This level of self-awareness and courage didn't happen overnight. In fact, it's been an evolving journey. For much of my life, I believed I wasn't enough: not brave enough, not smart enough, not important enough. The list was long. These beliefs were rooted in early life experiences and shaped the way I saw the world and my place within it.

I spent years in the grip of fear. I thought emotions happened *to* me. That people *made me* feel a certain way, angry, upset, frustrated. I lived as a victim of my emotional reactions, convinced that they had control over me, not the other way around. It wasn't until much later in life that I learned a fundamental truth: Emotions don't just happen to us, they're created by our thoughts.

That realization changed everything.

The Turning Point

In 2015, I attended a week-long personal development boot camp. It was brutal, raw, and transformational. Over the course of several days, I was stripped bare, emotionally, mentally, physically, and spiritually, and rebuilt with new understanding.

One exercise in particular left a lasting impression. We paired up with a partner and shared a painful childhood phrase - those words that had haunted us for years; you know *the* sentence. Things like: "You're a fat pig," or "You'll never amount to anything." Then, for one intense hour, we yelled these statements at each other.

Yes, it sounds extreme, even cruel, but it was designed with purpose.

It was within this carefully crafted experience when I came to the revolutionary realization that, "Emotions don't hurt me, they're just feedback." I realized they rise up and move through me like a wave, with a chemical release that lasts about six seconds, building to a crescendo (crest of the wave) and then ebbing away. The entire cycle takes approximately ninety seconds, as long as we *don't cling* to the emotions.

What emerged was a deep emotional release. Anger, shame, grief, rage, guilt; all of it came flooding out. And then… release. Letting go. For the first time, I understood that emotions were simply energy - waves that rise, crest, and fall. If I didn't cling to them, they passed. This knowledge gave me power and a new belief. I can now view emotions as feedback and signal information, not as threats.

This was the moment my understanding of Authentic Leadership fundamentally shifted. I realized I'd been afraid of my own emotions my entire life, convinced that feeling them meant weakness, that showing them meant I was losing.

Before this bootcamp, I was terrified of emotions. Terrified of being *too much* or *too emotional.* But since this time, I learned that emotions are not there to be feared but to be recognized, embraced, and allowed to pass through me.

They are there to guide us. They don't define us; they inform us.

When we learn to regulate our emotions, to dial them up or down as needed, we unlock one of the greatest superpowers of Authentic Leadership.

The Art Of Self-Regulation

Self-regulation is the second component of Authentic Leadership (after self-awareness). It's the conscious ability to recognize what state you are in emotionally, choose whether that state is serving you, and shift accordingly.

It's not about suppression. It's about calibration.

If I need to bring more empathy into a conversation, I now know how to access that part of myself. If I feel irritation creeping in, I have the ability to dial up and dial down (self-regulate). These are the tools that help you step back, reassess, and choose a different emotional response.

This is another moment where the *Three-Step NPC Formula* (Notice, Pause, Choose) comes into play - a framework that's transformed the way I navigate both challenges and triumphs. I used to think this was about compartmentalizing myself, but when you do that, you just create inner conflict and confusion. This is an absolutely exhausting way to live, and is never sustainable long-term. It's not about compartmentalizing yourself; it's about being fully integrated and congruent.

The Myth Of Compartmentalization

For many years, I believed that being a professional and a leader meant keeping my worlds separate. I had distinct personas: work Elizabeth, family Elizabeth, and friend Elizabeth. I curated each one carefully, believing this separation was not only necessary but admirable.

I became so adept at it, that a colleague was genuinely shocked to discover - after working together for three months - that I had children. This wasn't accidental; it was deliberate. I believed that in order to be taken seriously, I had to withhold parts of who I was. This rigid categorization to compartmentalize created what I now term *mental compartments and lies.*

What I didn't realize was the tremendous cost of this fragmentation. It was exhausting. I was constantly shape-shifting, adapting my personality, my behavior, even my values, depending on the context and who was around. I lost sight of who I truly was.

The incongruence between the roles I played and the person I actually was led to a collapse - physically, mentally, and emotionally.

In April 2002, my mind and body could no longer sustain the charade. The collapse was catastrophic. I burned out so severely that I could barely function. For three agonizing months, I couldn't perform even the most basic functions of daily living without assistance. I struggled every day to live and to breathe. Through a haze of medication, self-loathing, and pity, I dragged myself forward through what felt like thick mud. There were many times I felt like I wouldn't make it through, when I began to believe the falsehood that it would be easier for my family if I wasn't here, and I considered daily, how to ease *their* pain.

Those were dark days, filled with medication, tears, heartache, self-doubt, and a belief that my family would be better off without me. But through years of therapy, personal growth, and relentless determination, I began to rebuild.

It wasn't quick, and it wasn't easy, but it was a valuable gift I received. Today, more than two decades later, I live a life full of joy, purpose, and authenticity. I've been medication-free for over 14 years, and have never returned to that dark place again. I have never sunk into depression, even though they said I would always experience depressive episodes.

I've created a thriving authentic, blossoming, exciting life; free from medication, free from depression, free from panic attacks, free from self-judgement (most of the time, still up-leveling on this skill), free from the chains of the past, and free from the destructive belief that I am not allowed to be me.

I'm no longer shackled by the need for approval, nor do I wear the labels others tried to give me: *mentally unstable, depressive, broken, a victim.* I've shed them all, because I've done the inner work to lead myself first, I can now lead others with authenticity, integrity, and compassion.

The Ongoing Evolution

Authentic Leadership is not a destination. It's not a static state you achieve and then remain in forever. It's a living, breathing, evolving practice.

Every day, I learn something new about myself. Every day, I make tiny tweaks. Every day, I strive to become a little more congruent, a little more connected, a little more me. I continually explore with curiosity and openness, better ways of BEing, DOing, and HAVEing.

I still have moments of doubt. I still catch myself wondering if I'm too much or not enough. But those moments are now fleeting. I have the tool to rapidly shift from this BS into more self-empowering and congruent beliefs. They're no longer the soundtrack to my life.

They are simply echoes of an old story I no longer live by.

Leading From The Inside Out

Today, I lead with clarity, courage, and conviction. I'm aligned with my values. I'm transparent with my emotions. I don't hide behind roles or titles. I bring my whole self to every situation, strengths, realities, feelings, and all.

Authentic Leadership, for me, is about showing others what's possible when you choose to lead yourself first. When you dare to instigate self-awareness and self-regulation. When you dare to look inward, ask hard questions, and make aligned choices, even when it's scary.

So, to you who is reading this now, know this: You are not broken. You are not too much. You are not alone. You are simply evolving, just like I am. And in that evolution lies the power to lead authentically, from the inside out.

"The most powerful person in the room isn't the one who shouts the loudest, it's the one who knows themselves the deepest."
—*Christine Burns*

Christine

For me, Authentic Leadership is about showing up as my true self - no masks, no performance, no worrying about what others think I should be. It starts with leading myself first. If I can't lead myself with integrity and alignment, how on earth can I lead anyone else?

It's not about putting on a leadership *hat* and becoming someone I'm not. It's about being the best version of me - for *me* first - and then for the people I serve, support, and work alongside. It's about living and leading from the inside out.

I haven't always had this clarity. This idea has evolved for me over time.

Like most people, I used to think I had to tick certain boxes, fit a mold, or behave a certain way to be "seen" as a leader. But through my work and personal experiences (and thanks to the incredible framework of *Psychological Capital* that we teach in our trainings) I've come to realize that Authentic Leadership is about building and using four key inner resources: *Hope, Efficacy, Resilience,* and *Optimism.*

Let me walk you through how this has shown up in my journey.

Hope: Holding The Vision

Hope isn't wishful thinking. It's that deep belief that tomorrow can be better than today, and that I have the power and capacity to make it so. I don't always know *how* things will work out, but I absolutely know *they will.* I trust myself, my team, and the universe of support around me.

Hope is a guiding light. It's not passive; it's powerful.

One of the clearest examples of this was during my time managing a university department. The leadership above us had dropped away for various reasons, and suddenly we were left steering the ship ourselves. I didn't have all the answers, no one did. But we came together, mucked in, and had each other's backs. I didn't need to pretend to know everything. I allowed the team to bring their brilliance, and I brought mine.

That trust, in each other and in the process, was a massive act of hope in action.

Efficacy: Backing Myself

Self-efficacy is more than confidence. It's the unwavering belief in our ability to figure things out, to show up in our genius, and to take the next step, even when we have no clue what that step looks like yet.

I remember moving from New Zealand to Australia for a new university role. I didn't know the systems. I was in unfamiliar territory. But I knew my content, I knew how to connect with students, and I knew I could learn whatever I needed to.

So I asked questions. I showed up. I backed myself.

That belief didn't mean I felt certain every second - far from it - but I knew I had what it takes to figure it out. That's the ripple effect of efficacy. When I back myself, others start backing themselves too. Teams rise together when individuals own their strengths.

Resilience: Bouncing Forward

Now, let's be honest about *Resilience.* I don't buy into the idea of just *bouncing back.* That suggests going back to how things were; same thinking, same patterns, same old same.

No thanks.

For me (and us), resilience in Authentic Leadership means *bouncing forward.* It's about moving through adversity and coming out stronger, smarter, and more solid on the other side. It's choosing to learn from the BS, whether that's Belief Systems, Blind Spots, or good old-fashioned Bullsh*t.

This is what *antifragility* is all about - a concept from Nassim Taleb that goes beyond resilience. The resilient resist shock and stay the same; the antifragile grow stronger through challenge.[10] I've experienced this over and over again - in leadership, in sport, and in life.

---

[10] Taleb NN. Antifragile: Things That Gain from Disorder. New York: Random House; 2012.

Take my hockey career. I burst onto the scene quickly, and people said, "You haven't done your time. You can't progress that fast." They believed in a fixed process. I didn't. I kept showing up, even after knockbacks. I was told I was the best goalie in the country, and still didn't get selected for the Olympics.

Did it hurt? Of course. But I chose to keep learning, to grow from it. That's *Resilience* with a capital *R*. Not because I endured it, but because I evolved through it.

Optimism: Choosing A Better Lens

People often confuse optimism with fake positivity. Let me be clear - positivity is BS, as it's pretending everything's fine when it's not. I'm all about *realism first*, then choosing to see opportunity. That's what true *optimism* is - a grounded belief that, even when things are tough, there's a way through.

I live by Winston Churchill's quote: *"A pessimist sees the difficulty in every opportunity; an optimist sees the opportunity in every difficulty."*

Optimism doesn't mean denying hardship. It means acknowledging the hard, the fear, the anger - calling it what it is - then consciously choosing a meaning that moves us forward.

When I was diagnosed via a phone call with endometrial cancer in November 2016, I didn't pretend it was fine. My first reaction was very real, including a whole lot of F-bombs and disbelief.

But within seconds, something shifted. I tapped into my inner certainty and said, "Right, I'll do my thing mentally, emotionally, physically, and spiritually, and you, the medical team, do your thing. Together we'll knock this bastard off."

That's trained antifragility. That's Optimism in action. It's not a mindset I was born with, it's a muscle I've built, day in and day out, through sport, leadership, and coaching.

The Truth About Positivity And Emotion

At WALT Institute, we teach that it's okay to call something *sh*t* when it is. That's not negative, that's honest.

Eckhart Tolle refers to this as *isness*. It's the ability to call things as they are. Not sugar-coating. Not denial. Naming it, and from there, choosing how to respond.[11]

The most powerful leaders I've met are those who embrace the full spectrum of human emotion. Because here's the truth: *You can't have happiness without sadness, or love without grief.*

When we allow ourselves to feel it all, we gain influence in teams, in relationships, and in life. The person with the broadest range of emotions is the person with the most flexibility and authentic power in any situation.

Evolving Leadership

Authentic Leadership is not a destination. It's not something we *achieve* and tick off. It's ongoing. I still have a coach - I'll always have a coach - because I believe there's always another level.

Psychological Capital, that combination of hope, efficacy, resilience, and optimism, is the framework that supports me to lead well. To lead in alignment. To lead with heart, grit, and honesty. To lead as me.

Whether I'm working with a team, in a business, with a client, or just navigating life, this way of being works. It keeps me grounded, evolving, and connected to something greater than ego.

That's Authentic Leadership, and it's available to each one of us.

---

[11] Tolle E. *Stillness Speaks.* Novato (CA): New World Library; 2003.

What Has Authentic Leadership Taught You About Yourself That You Didn't Expect To Learn?

A Life I Never Thought Possible

Elizabeth

If you'd told me years ago that I'd be living a vibrant, joyful, fulfilling life, filled with color, laughter, and an overwhelming sense of freedom, I would have laughed in disbelief. That kind of life? For me? Never. I didn't think it was even on the menu. I never imagined I could be the one to create it, shape it, and live it.

Back then, the idea that I had a choice seemed absurd. A choice in how I thought, how I felt, and how I responded to the world around me. The notion that I could consciously choose my mood, my reactions, my next step - that I could get over and through challenges with both speed and ease - was completely foreign. But here I am.

Authentic Leadership changed everything.

It's given me more than just tools, it's handed me the reins. I get to choose how I *BE* in the world. That's not just empowering, it's liberating. I laugh, daily. I explore the unknown with curiosity instead of fear. I live with an inner freedom I once thought belonged only to other people. That freedom is now mine, because I chose to show up as me; unapologetically, courageously, and consistently.

One of the most surprising and powerful lessons along the way has been realizing that I have agency. Not just in the big, dramatic life moments, but in every tiny, seemingly insignificant moment too. Every micro-moment is a chance to choose. And I do. I now meet life's challenges with clarity, grace, and agility. Adversity still shows up - it always will - but I'm no longer at its mercy, and it shows up less and less. I move through it, around it, rise above it. I am not consumed by it.

The ripple effects of this way of living have been extraordinary. I never imagined the magnitude of opportunities that would unfold when I stepped into my authentic self - The people I've met, the global connections I've made, or the privilege I've gained to lead others and influence thousands of lives. I'm giving them the skills and confidence to live with authenticity, too.

That's the real gift - the impact that we can have when we choose to lead from who we truly are.

And it all began with a decision. A decision to show up, be real, and reclaim my life. It's a life that I never thought was possible, yet now it's one that I live fully, every single day.

Learning to consciously choose my thoughts, emotions, and actions - developing that deep self-awareness and the ability to self-regulate - was the turning point. It laid the groundwork for everything that followed. Once I understood that I wasn't just reacting to life but actively shaping it, I could finally begin to build something stronger within myself.

That internal shift became the launchpad for what came next: *Psychological Capital.*

Psychological Capital: A New Foundation For Living

The next vital component of Authentic Leadership is *Psychological Capital.* It's not just a fancy phrase; it's a way of *being.* Psychological capital consists of four elements:

- Hope
- Efficacy
- Resilience
- Optimism

These aren't fluffy ideals or *positive thinking* platitudes. They are evidence-based, deeply rooted belief systems that can be cultivated by anyone.

Yes, even those of us who thought Psychological Capital was only for *other* people. I used to think these traits were reserved for people with easier childhoods or fewer emotional scars. But I've since learned otherwise. I've grown these traits from the inside out, through consistent practice, deep reflection, and radical honesty. And now they're part of who I am.

Hope: Anchored In Possibility

Let's start with *hope*. Not the flimsiness of *hoping*. True hope, as psychologist Barbara Fredrickson describes, arises not in easy times but in uncertainty. Hope is what we feel when things are unclear, but we still believe in possibility. It opens us up. It clears away the fear and helps us see new solutions. *"Hope is not just a positive emotion; it arises when circumstances are dire and improvement is uncertain but possible... allowing us to become more creative and inspired to solve problems."*[12]

Hope is a belief system. It's the inner voice that says, "No matter what, I will find a way." Before embracing Authentic Leadership, I didn't know I could have that. I used to give up easily, hand over control to circumstances. Now, I stand in hope every day, with the evidence of my own resilience as proof.

Efficacy: Rewriting Your Inner Narrative

Next comes *efficacy*. This is about my belief in my own abilities. I never used to have much of it, but I learned this was just a *pattern*. A pattern of thinking and behaving. Albert Bandura (the grandfather researcher of self-efficacy) defines self-efficacy as: *"Beliefs in one's capabilities to organise and execute the course of action required to produce given attainments."*[13]

---

[12] Fredrickson BL. *Positivity: Groundbreaking research reveals how to embrace the hidden strength of positive emotions, overcome negativity, and thrive.* New York: Crown Publishers/Random House; 2009.

[13] Bandura A. *Self-efficacy: The exercise of control.* New York (NY): W. H. Freeman; 1997.

This belief didn't come naturally to me. I used to see myself as less capable, less worthy, less everything. But as I learned to lead authentically, I realized I had the power to shift that story. I began to *choose* how I would interpret situations. I grew my confidence one decision, one belief, one action at a time, until I have rewritten my inner narrative, and continue to do so every day.

Efficacy is not about arrogance or bravado, it's about grounded, inner certainty. It's knowing that I can trust myself, no matter what. That I will figure it out. That I've got my own back.

Resilience: The Bounce Forward

I always thought I wasn't resilient. I thought that was something I lacked. Until I looked back and realized, *I've come through hell and I'm still standing.* That's resilience. But even more than that, I've learned to *bounce forward,* not just back.

Resilience is often described as the ability to bounce back; however, as Christine has already said, I don't know about you but I certainly do *not* want to just bounce back. Why would I want to bounce back to the same struggle, the same limiting beliefs, the same old emotional patterns? Why would I want to bounce back to the same shitty situation? The same shitty thoughts, emotions, and results I had before I hit the tough stuff?

I want to bounce *FORWARD.* Moving to a different point, creating a different outcome, learning, growing, expanding, fine-tuning, celebrating, and BEing in a different place than where I just was before. Resilience, in the context of Authentic Leadership, is about *growing* through what you go through. It's evolution. *"Resilience is the capacity of a system to adapt successfully to significant challenges that threaten its function, viability, or development."*[14]

---

[14] Masten AS. Resilience theory and research on children and families: Past, present, and promise. *J Fam Theory Rev.* 2018;10(1):12–31.

Imagine a tall bamboo plant in a windstorm; bending, twisting, never breaking. That's the kind of adaptability I've cultivated. I can shift, flex, and realign without being uprooted. Every challenge now becomes an opportunity to grow. This mindset is not something I ever expected to learn, but now, I can't imagine life without it.

Optimism: A Muscle I Learned To Flex

I, like a large percentage of the population, am a natural pessimist. My default is to anticipate the worst, to assume things will be too hard or too painful, but Authentic Leadership has taught me that *optimism* is a *choice*. It's a learned pattern of thought. As Martin Seligman puts it: *"Optimism is a matter of how you interpret the setbacks and reversals in your life."*[15]

Optimism is an attitude you choose, a pattern you train, which can significantly impact your level of subject well-being, satisfaction and happiness.[16]

Optimism is not naivety. It's not ignoring reality, it's saying: *Even if this is hard, I believe something good can still come of it.* It's trusting that the effort I put in leads to a great outcome. Those setbacks are temporary, not permanent. That I get to choose how I interpret what's happening around me, and within me.

This simple shift has radically changed my life. Not because I now wear rose-tinted glasses or pretend everything is okay when it is not, but because I've trained my brain to notice, pause, align with my purpose, and believe in myself.

---

[15] Seligman MEP. *Learned optimism.* New York: Pocket Books; 1998.

[16] Diener E, Chan MY. Happy people live longer: Subjective well-being contributes to health and longevity. *Appl Psychol Health Well Being.* 2011;3(1):1–43.

The Three 'B.S.'s: Blind Spots, Belief Systems, and... You Know the Rest

Of course, this journey hasn't been without its challenges. Authentic Leadership has also taught me to confront the three big B.S.'s that hold us back:

1. *Blind Spots* – We can't change what we can't see. That's why I always work with a coach and am a coach. Self-awareness is a superpower, and sometimes we need someone else to point out the things we're too close to notice.

2. *Belief Systems* – We often carry the belief that *this is just the way I am.* But neuroscience, epigenetics, and my lived experience tell us otherwise. We can *recode* our thinking, retrain our habits, and shift our identity from the inside out.

3. *Bullsh*t* – Yes, the classic. The stories we tell ourselves, the excuses, the justifications. That's just our little critter brain trying to keep us safe. But *safe* isn't where growth lives. Growth requires being uncomfortable, having courage, taking action, and embracing a willingness to call out our own B.S.

You Have This Power Too

This journey, this becoming, has changed everything. And what's more, it's available to you, too. I've learned to wake up each morning and choose. Choose what I focus on, and choose who I show up as.

I choose to lead. I choose to create. I choose to embody hope, efficacy, resilience, and optimism. Not with the BS of perfection, not with the unrealistic belief that I will never falter. But I choose to show up consistently, courageously, and confidently to be the very best version of me that I can be.

Authentic Leadership didn't just teach me how to lead others, it taught me how to lead myself.

Christine

Honestly? I didn't expect the biggest lesson to be about ME. I thought leadership would be all about strategy, structure, systems, the *playbook* stuff. But what I've learned is that I don't have to fit into what a textbook says, or fit the traditional leadership box, and I don't have to do leadership the way other people do it. Authentic Leadership is an *inside job*. It's not about the drills and the hustle, it's about who you *are* when the pressure's on, when the game changes at the last minute, and when no one's watching. I get to show up in my own values and beliefs, and what aligns with me.

I used to think I had to toughen up, hold back, and keep it polished and professional. But the real game-changer was discovering that my strength is actually in showing up *as me* - raw, real, and unfiltered. I don't need to pretend I've got it all sorted. I don't need to run someone else's plays. I get to bring *my* style to the field, the boardroom, and the stage.

And guess what? That's when the results started landing.

The turning point for me was when I stepped into being the CEO of our business, WALT Institute. The biggest shift happened when I fully embraced what Elizabeth and my coach, Linda, said to me: *"Lead in a way that aligns with you. Treat your team like a sports team. Lead in the moment. Be you!"* I realized this way of leading was my natural *know-how* and *go-to* state. This is how I lead best as an Authentic Leader.

What surprised me most was how powerful it is to *own my space*. To speak straight. To lead with heart, with guts, and with presence. To drop the mask and just *be*. Authentic Leadership has shown me that I don't need to tick every box or follow the crowd. I get to lead with *conviction*, with *courage*, and with the kind of *consistency* that comes from being rock-solid in who I am.

You don't learn that from a course or a manual. That's reps. That's training. That's consistently showing up for yourself, day in and day out, no matter what the scoreboard says. That's where the genius kicks in - when you lead from your BEing, you empower others to step up too. You inspire, influence, and ignite your team to believe in themselves. That's how high-performing teams are built.

So, what's the greatest lesson Authentic Leadership taught me? That *being me* - fully, fiercely, and unapologetically - is my superpower in leadership. It's not about doing more, it's about being *more you.* A true Authentic Leader cultivates their DOing from who they are BEing. Because Authentic Leadership is about you as a whole person, not you as a multiple personality, compartmentalized, boxed-in, rule-following robot.

It's about bringing your whole self - your strengths, your smarts, your spark - to the game. Every day. Every play. I get to be me, bringing my own genius every day, and that's a play I'll run every damn day.

Has There Been A Moment When You Almost Gave Up, But Didn't? What Kept You Going?

Elizabeth

There have been many moments when giving up felt like the only option. One I've already shared in this chapter - when my mental health was hanging by a thread. Another, when my 22-year marriage fell apart. Another, when the contract for my dream job was ripped out from under me, just two weeks before I was due to move countries to start it. And another, perhaps one of the most raw and humbling, in the early days of building our business.

Christine and I were doing everything we knew how to do. Long hours. Creating content. Teaching. Showing up for people. Hustling hard. But despite all the effort, things weren't working - at least, not financially.

I remember one day looking at our bank account and seeing $2.52. We still had 12 days until the next income came in. No savings. No investments to fall back on, because we'd already invested every cent into our vision. On top of that, we were more than $150,000 in debt. We couldn't even afford a bar of soap, let alone groceries.

I found myself making excuses to work from home, not because I needed the flexibility, but because I couldn't afford the petrol or train ticket to get to the office. Things looked bleak. I was tired. Drained. It felt like no matter how much we gave, it just wasn't enough. I thought, *Why are we doing this? Why are we sacrificing so much to serve others when we can't even look after ourselves?* The idea of going back to a steady full-time job, a role that was *fine* but never aligned with my true purpose, started to feel tempting.

But then I remembered who I am.

In that moment - when walking away seemed easier than staying the course - I paused and reconnected with my *why*. I remembered that I am not here to live a life of compromise or play small. I am here to lead with authenticity, to make an impact, and to create change from the inside out. Giving up would have meant betraying the vision that had already transformed my own life and was beginning to ripple out to others.

So instead of folding, I chose to rise. Not with blind optimism, but with fierce commitment and clarity. I stopped doing for the sake of doing and started *being* the leader I know I am. That choice, to stand in my truth, even when everything felt uncertain, is what kept me going, and is what still fuels me today.

Christine

I'm not a *giver upper*. Never have been. Sure, there have been moments that slowed me down, moments where I had to pause, breathe, regroup, and ask, *Alright, what needs to shift here? What do we need to do differently to pivot this situation, the business or change direction?* But giving up? That's *not* in my playbook!

What keeps me going is my unshakable optimism. It's not blind hope, it's deeply wired into me. That mindset started early. Growing up, one of Mum's go-to lines was: *There's always a way.* And that has always stuck.

I've carried that belief with me on every pitch, every turf, every stage, every challenge. I might have muttered, *How the hell do I get through this?* a few times, but the intention has always been: *Keep moving forward.* Even if it's a shuffle, a step, or a side-step, it's movement forward and movement creates momentum.

It starts with this belief that I have: *There's always a way* and there's always a different environment, person, thought pattern, or framework that I can tap into.

Now, don't get me wrong, I'm not talking about smashing my head against a brick wall and hoping it'll fall down. I don't believe in burning yourself out for the sake of stubbornness. It's not about pushing forward blindly. It's about finding a different approach, a different person, a new environment, or a mindset to tap into.

It's not chasing, it's *purposeful discovery.* That's the key. That's what keeps me in the leadership game.

People get stuck thinking they have to know the *how* before they start. But the truth is, *the how catches up.* The *how* catches up because action creates information, momentum, and opportunities you simply can't see from the sidelines. We must trust ourselves and begin taking action with a belief in ourselves. Trust the process. Trust *yourself.*

My largest test of not giving up was when I was lecturing at a University in Melbourne. I could see the cracks in the system and feel the weight of outdated, ego-driven leadership. Every time I brought fresh ideas or a new approach, I got the same tired answer: "We've always done it this way." But I knew it could be better, not just for me, but for the students. I kept pushing myself to show up every day and do my best.

Even though physically I was having huge medical issues for many months, I kept pushing. That fight wasn't about ego; it was about evolution of processes and systems for the benefit of the students. Eventually, I didn't have a choice.

When I was diagnosed with cancer back in 2016, my body forced me to stop. It took me out, hard. I had to completely step away from my work. I didn't know what was coming next. I had no map, no clear outcome. But I knew one thing: I knew I would find a way. I knew that I would give it my absolute best shot.

I wasn't doing this to prove anything, but rather I believed in showing up fully. No matter what. And if things didn't turn out how I hoped? It wouldn't be because I didn't give it everything I had, or that I just gave up. That's the difference between giving up and giving your all.

We must trust ourselves and begin taking action with self-belief first. Because leadership isn't about sticking to one rigid path, it's about knowing there's *always* another way. It's about aligning with your strengths, tapping into your genius, and staying open to what's possible, even when the scoreboard looks rough.

So yeah, I'm not a giver-upper. I'm a re-thinker. A re-framer. A relentless believer in limitless possibilities. When things get tough, I don't drop out, I *dig in*. I shift gears. I create the next play. I adapt, and I keep going. That's what Authentic Leadership demands: *Back yourself, dream bigger, and always find a way.*

What Do You Come Back To When Everything Feels Uncertain?

Elizabeth

I come back to *me*. Not the version of me that's panicked or spiraling or trying to control everything. I come back to the grounded, centered, ever-evolving version of me. The one who leads with awareness, courage, and choice.

The work I've done to develop Authentic Leadership - to truly understand myself, to regulate my emotions, to choose how I respond - has changed everything. I used to sit in the discomfort of uncertainty for days, sometimes weeks. It felt paralyzing.

Now? Those moments last less than five minutes, because I've trained myself to recognize them for what they are: A signal, not a sentence.

Uncertainty used to unnerve me. I liked structure, predictability, and knowing what's coming next. I clung to planning, to certainty, because it made me feel safe. So when the unknown crept in, it would throw me completely off balance. I'd react. I'd stress. I'd often project that onto others.

I genuinely believed I couldn't be flexible, couldn't find another way. I saw only roadblocks, but over time, I've learned to see uncertainty differently. Not as a threat, but as a portal. A space of potential. Because within it lies possibility, creativity, and growth. I don't have to control the outcome; I get to choose how I show up in the moment. And that is always within my power.

So, when things feel chaotic, whether it's a tech meltdown at a major event, or the tough decision to let a team member go, I come back to my internal home. I come back to the clarity of who I *choose* to be in that moment.

And I don't rely on willpower alone. I activate my Psychological Capital.

Hope reminds me there's something better ahead. Efficacy tells me I've done hard things before, and I can do them again. Resilience helps me bounce, not just back but forward. And optimism lights the way, even if only a few steps at a time.

Coming back to myself is the anchor. It's strength. It's stability. It's a deep breath in the middle of the storm. And when I do that, without judgment of self, I get to lead from a place of authenticity, vulnerability, and truth.

That's what keeps me going. That's how I walk through uncertainty, again and again.

Christine

I like uncertainty. Honestly, I thrive in uncertainty. It's not something I avoid; it's something I embrace. I don't need all the answers up front. I don't need to have it all mapped out. What I do need is to back myself, because I know, without a doubt, I'll figure it out.

Uncertainty is actually one of my top human needs. That surprises a lot of people, because most of us crave certainty. Most of us want predictability, safety, and control. But for me, uncertainty equals fun and growth. It equals variety, adventure, and possibility. It means there's room for something unexpected and often extraordinary to show up.

That's not to say uncertainty is easy. It can be uncomfortable. Messy. Stretchy. But for me, it's exciting, expansive, and filled with opportunity. This is a choice, and what I come back to. It's what keeps me grounded when everything else feels up in the air.

What helps me hold that space is my Psychological Capital:

- **Hope**: I don't have to know exactly *how*, but I believe there's *always* a way forward.
- **Efficacy**: I back myself to find a way.
- **Resilience**: I know I'll bounce forward, not just back.
- **Optimism**: I genuinely believe the future holds something better.

This internal foundation is what I tap into, especially when the external world gets shaky. It's not a strategy, it's a way of being. It's mindset in action, and I live it every day.

When I was training through Robbins Research International's Coaching Academy - one of the most stretching, unpredictable, and growth-packed experiences of my life - I faced uncertainty every single day. For three intense months, we never knew what was coming next. No hint of what challenge, conversation, or curveball we'd be thrown into. Add to that the time zone chaos of doing the training overnight in Australia, the intensity of the work, and the emotional and mental demands? Well, it was the ultimate test.

But you know what? I loved it.

Not because it was easy, it absolutely wasn't. But because every single day, I got to step into uncertainty with courage and curiosity. I got to trust myself. I got to see what I was made of. I wasn't just learning about leadership - I was living it. In real time. In the arena.

That's the thing about uncertainty: It reveals your mindset. It shows you where you stand when the path disappears. And if your mindset is strong, grounded, and trained, you don't crumble. You get creative. You get clear. You adapt. You stay in the game.

Here's what I've learned over and over: *The how catches up.* If you keep moving, keep showing up, keep backing yourself, you'll always find a way. There's **always** a way. So when the world feels uncertain, when the business takes a hit, when a curveball diagnosis lands, when the ground shifts beneath me, what do I come back to?

I come back to belief. I come back to courage. I come back to me. Authentic Leadership doesn't need guarantees or wait for the path to be perfect, it leads into the unknown, and it thrives in the uncertainty.

The best part that you, who are reading this right now, need to know about is this: *You* can train for this level of authenticity. *You* can strengthen this skill. Just like building a muscle, *you* get to build *your* capacity for uncertainty by doing something new every day.

Step out of your comfort zone *on purpose.*

Start with something small, the little unknowns. Go a different way to work. Eat a different food. Learn something new. Have a conversation with a stranger that stretches you. That's how you expand your skills and your mindset. You get to build the repetitions that matter. When you train your mindset, you don't just survive the uncertainty, you own it.

By doing the little things, you are creating deeper neurological pathways of authenticity, which then create new beliefs, which then strengthen your new approach, your new attitude, your new mindset. By making these tiny tweaks and then celebrating your progress, you then optimize your growth and new perspective.

This is *Mindset*: The Mindset of an Authentic Leader, and that's exactly where we're going next.

When we step back and look at the bigger picture of our journeys that we have shared above, marked by setbacks, self-discovery, resilience, and deep personal growth, Elizabeth and I have come to realize that Authentic Leadership isn't a destination. It's a way of *being*.

It's about owning who we are, even when the path gets messy. It's about choosing courage over comfort and coming home to ourselves in the face of uncertainty. What we have both discovered is the level of agency we have developed - the unwavering belief that we *can* choose our thoughts, shift our emotional state, and take purposeful action no matter what is happening around us.

Authentic Leadership has rewired how we see ourselves, our teams, and the world. It has given us the tools to redefine meaning, sharpen our focus, and align our beliefs and actions with who we truly are. And that is the power of perception. As we step into the next chapter, we invite you to explore the foundation that underpins all of this - *Mindset*. Because how we *think* determines what we *see*, and what we *see* shapes what we *believe* is possible.

Chapter Takeaways:

Lead Yourself First – Any result begins with mastering your internal world *first*. You must lead yourself *before* you lead others.

Values Alignment – Integrity and truth are the compass points of Authentic Leadership. Alignment builds trust.

Compass and Steering Wheel – Self-awareness shows the direction; self-regulation keeps you on course.

Emotions as Feedback – Emotions aren't threats; they are data that informs you something needs your attention.

Drop the Mask – Authentic Leadership requires honesty and vulnerability. People trust what's real, not what's perfect.

Authenticity Over Approval – Stop people-pleasing and start showing up as your true self.

Integration Over Compartmentalization – Bring your whole self to every space; authenticity thrives in wholeness.

Freedom from External Approval – True confidence comes when you approve of yourself.

Challenges are Growth – Difficult experiences are opportunities to evolve, not obstacles to avoid.

Unlock Possibility - There is *always* a way. You get to choose.

Radical Honesty – Call things as they are, *as is*. Honesty clears space for choice, authentic growth, and courage.

Adversity Builds Strength – Growth happens because of the storm, not despite it.

Process, Not Outcome – Authentic Leadership is a daily discipline, not a finish line. Commit to the process.

The Three B.S.'s – Notice your Belief Systems, Blind Spots, and Bullsh*t then choose what comes next, from an empowering space.

Legacy of *BEing* – The impact you leave is not what you did or the results you got, it is who you were *BEing* in the moment.

Section Two - DOing

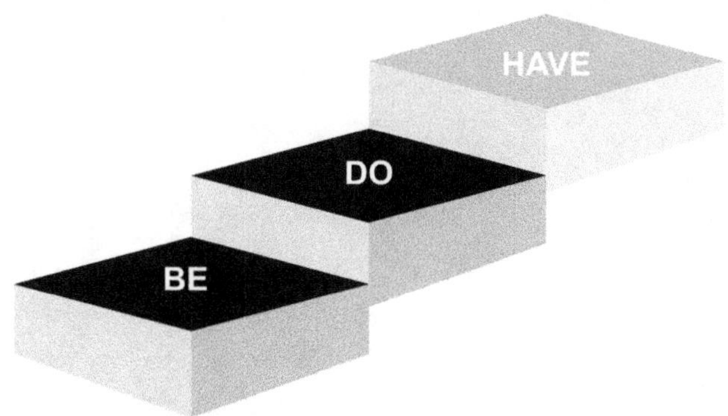

Thinking and dreaming are essential, but without DOing, nothing changes. We can gather all the knowledge, read all the books, and attend all the workshops, but without action we will still be in the exact same place, in six months, 12 months, even 12 years from now.

This is the essence of **agency***; the ability to take intentional action, persist in the face of challenges, and consciously design the life and leadership you choose. Agency is not about waiting for the perfect timing, the ideal conditions, or having complete certainty. It is about moving forward despite discomfort, resistance, or fear.*

We know this to be true as we have both lived this. It was only when we took consistent daily action - the next small step again and again - that we began to see the transformation. Momentum built, growth happened, and impact unfolded.

In the next three chapters, you will discover how to break free from the patterns that hold you back, cultivate the mindset that fuels courageous action, and master the art of agency. Because Authentic Leadership isn't about what you know, it's proven, lived and experienced, through what you do.

Your future isn't waiting. It's created through action. Let's go.

CHAPTER 4

Own It – The Mindset Of Agency And Authentic Leadership

"Unless you do something, you're not going to get something. You go further by action and activity, not just by thinking."
—*Joseph McClendon III*

Agency – The Skill Of Doing: Why Some People Take Action And Others Don't

Elizabeth

I walk up the stairs to the stage. I've just been introduced as the next speaker at the Brisbane International Health Conference. I pause behind the curtain, out of sight of the audience, and I can see some of them sitting in their seats, eyes fixed on the stage.

This is it. This is the moment I have worked towards for the last three decades of my life.

In that moment I realized I have moved forward from being a person who hated speaking in front of others, who flushed with embarrassment, mumbled her words, thought she was never enough. A person who had incredible tension and nervousness in her stomach that almost made her throw up.

This is the moment I have worked towards, practiced for, dreamed of, and created. As I hear my name being called, I step onto the stage with confidence, certainty, and excitement.

This is not arrogance, ego, or seeking to have power over the audience. This is stepping into my true authentic potential of who I am and sharing my unique message to inspire the audience so that they will take one tiny step forward. Another step towards creating their best life.

Every moment that followed was magic. I connected. I crafted. I built genuine rapport with the audience, not to impress them, but to *inspire and influence* from a place of truth. I shared parts of myself with openness and vulnerability, offering strategies they could embed in their own lives. I felt completely present. Grounded, grateful, and alive in my purpose.

As I brought it all together at the end, I left them with one powerful question: "What's the one tiny tweak you'll take from today to make your leadership, and your life, even better?"

This was amazing. I felt so confident, clear on my message, and proud of myself for stepping up, and stepping into my authentic self.

This, like anything we create in our lives, is the product of *action*. Taking consistent daily action towards our end goals and targets, no matter what. No matter what the weather, how we feel, how much money we have, or how much support we have. The list is endless.

In this and the next two chapters, we will challenge the patterns that hold us back and stop us from taking action, and share proven techniques to bust through them, so you can experience a powerful internal shift. You get to become the leader who *always takes considered action* and who *has the courage to be disliked and lead authentically*. Because what you say you are, you are!

If you want to create your future and design the life you choose, then you get to take action and master the art and science of *agency*!

Agency refers to "an individual's capacity to take intentional action, exert control over their environment, and persist in goal-directed behavior, particularly in the face of challenges" (Snyder, 2002,). Simply put, it is the individual's ability to initiate and sustain actions over time to achieve the desired outcome they set out to achieve. This means the person (you) has developed the ability to keep going regardless of any self-doubt, physical factors, environmental factors, or any other influences that may crop up. This is about your mindset, the one that you *choose* every single day.[17]

MINDSET – The Master Key To Authentic Leadership

Mindset is the foundation of why we do what we do. It's not just what we think, it's *how* we think about ourselves, others, and the world we live in. Our mindset is our mental operating system, influencing everything from our mood and focus to the stories we tell ourselves.

Have you ever been anxious, confident, curious, critical, or deeply engaged? These are all different states of mind. But here's the kicker - we're not always aware of which *state* we're operating from. Much of our thinking is subconscious, driven by old experiences, beliefs, patterns, and values imprinted from our past. That means our actions are often reactions, not conscious choices, but automatic habits shaped by what was, rather than what is.

When we operate from a past-driven mindset, we filter the present through blame, shame, guilt, and judgment. It's like trying to drive forward while staring in the rearview mirror. It is possible for short periods of time, but not sustainable or effective! We miss the opportunities right in front of us. I see this constantly in leaders, athletes, and professionals who are physically present but mentally stuck in old loops of self-doubt, fear, or limitation.

Living in the present with an outdated mindset creates internal conflict and external chaos. If I don't build my mindset and authentic identity, then the conflict and chaos will own me. That's why the most powerful shift you can make as a leader is to consciously, purposefully, and intentionally choose your mindset.

---

[17] Snyder CR, Lopez SJ, editors. *Handbook of positive psychology.* Oxford: Oxford University Press; 2002.

Joseph McClendon III, a world-renowned neuropsychologist from the Neuro-Encoding Institute and a legend in the personal development and high-performance world, breaks down the mindset-performance connection into four words: *Think, Feel, Do, Have.*

"As I think, so I feel. As I feel, so I do. As I do, so I have."[18]

So simple. So powerful. If you don't like what you currently *have,* check what you *do.* What you *do* is shaped by how you *feel.* And how you *feel* is driven by what you *think.* Want better outcomes? Uplevel your thoughts. Shift your mindset.

Remember that *you don't have to believe every thought that crosses your mind.* Most of those thoughts are totally made up anyway. We make meaning of everything that happens. We choose the meaning and create a story around it, which becomes what we believe.

So why not make up better ones? Your mind will believe whatever story you tell it. Tell yourself a story/narrative that lifts you up instead of keeping you small. Mindset is personal.

We view the world and the experiences we have through our own lens. This lens is a combination of our experiences, beliefs, values, and the environment we were brought up in. Our mindset is shaped by our past, but it doesn't have to be *defined* by it. Two people can face the same event, say, an ice bath at 5 am, and have completely different experiences. One sees resilience, discipline, and growth. The other sees discomfort, sacrifice, and resistance.

The only difference? *Mindset.*

---

[18] McClendon JM III. About – The Neuroencoding Institute. 2025 [cited 2025 Nov 21]. Available from: https://www.neuroencoding.com/about/

What You Choose To Focus On Is Your Superpower.

What you focus on, you feel. What you feel, you act on. And what you act on determines your results. The brain's reticular activating system (RAS), your personal radar, proves this. A network of neurons located in the brainstem, your RAS is crucial for regulating arousal, wakefulness, and attention.

Once you decide something matters, your RAS goes hunting for more of it. It's like when you buy a new car and suddenly everyone's driving that same make and model. That's your RAS filtering your reality through what you *choose* to focus on.

When you focus on lack, you'll find it everywhere. When you focus on possibilities, they start showing up more. Think about your workplace. Does the energy feel stuck, slow, and heavy? Is the dominant narrative "We can't do this," "That won't work," or "It's always been this way, so it won't change"? If so, the mindset is focusing on and locked in scarcity. The RAS is stuck scanning for everything that is broken, wrong, and bad, and it will find it.

Wow, this type of focus and meaning creates a heavy, gloomy, low-spirited, depressing environment to be in, and therefore has the likelihood of pulling your mindset into a dark and negative place.

Now let's flip the script. What if the collective mindset shifted to:

- "What *can* we do?"
- "What do we *have*?"
- "What's possible *now*?"

This is the power of an *uplifted, Authentic Leadership mindset.* It shifts the focus and creates momentum, such as ongoing movement towards the outcomes you are creating. Creating a much richer life in every way. So what does it take to create your own Authentic Leadership mindset that has you focusing on what serves you, things you *can do*, and *do have*?

Christine

This got me thinking as I sat down to write this chapter, so I'll share this example with you. I was able to sit down with Elizabeth to scope out this chapter on paper and write down the framework I use to create my mindset. My response to her was, "I have no idea what the steps are, I just do it."

So, in true Elizabeth form, she asked me great questions, and here is the exact method I use.

This *Mindset Reset Method* is for you, so you can use the same method to create your own authentic mindset and switch into this, real fast. These five steps are my personal go-to strategy. I've used them throughout my life in elite sport, during terrifying moments in cancer treatment, when moving cities, starting new jobs, and standing in rooms I didn't feel ready for. I have trained myself by taking consistent action, growing the muscle, and now it's become second nature. I had to train for it, just like you can do now.

Remember: How you do *one* thing, is how you do *everything*. If you give up, throw a tantrum, or complain along the way, then that is showing you the pattern you have for everything you *do* in your life.

The MINDSET RESET Method:

5 Steps To Train Your Mindset For Any Challenge

1. Notice the Similarities

Unfamiliar doesn't mean unsafe. Your brain craves familiarity, so give it safety.

Ask: *What does this new thing remind me of? What parts have I done before?*
You may be meeting new people or entering a new space, but recognize that you've introduced yourself before. You've handled nerves before.

You've navigated uncertainty before. Find the thread of sameness and anchor yourself to it.

2. Be in a Great State

Your body speaks louder than your thoughts. Your body language sends signals to your brain about how you're feeling and operating (mindset). If you have poor posture, it creates poor emotions and a negative mindset. Change your posture (physiology), and you shift your body chemistry. Stand tall, breathe deep, move with purpose.

Amy Cuddy's "Power Pose" research shows how this physical reset boosts testosterone (muscularity, strength, and improved mood) by up to 20%, reduces cortisol (our stress hormone) down 25%, and increases risk-taking confidence by 33%. Even though some of these research statistics have since been questioned, Elizabeth and I have experienced and seen the impact of training people to stand tall, being centered and strong in their ability to engage their best self and to be more courageous. Want a strong mindset? **Start with your stance.**[19]

3. Identify What You Do Know and Can Do

Focus on your knowns, not your unknowns. Ask yourself: "What can I already do? What do I already have? What do I already know?"

For example, you may be going for a job interview on public transport to a building you have not been to before, to be interviewed by people you have not met before.

Some of the questions I would ask you to identify specifically what you do know and can do are:

- Have you used public transport before?
- Can you see this building or the area on a map?

---

[19] Carney DR, Cuddy AJC, Yap AJ. Power posing: Brief nonverbal displays affect neuroendocrine levels and risk tolerance. *Psychol Sci.* 2010;21(10):1363–8.

- Have you had any interview-type situations before? Do you know your strengths and soft spots for this role?
- Can you do at least 50% of the role?

Yes, yes, yes, and *yes.*

Every "yes" builds momentum and confidence. The more you tap into what you already *can do*, the more you rewire your brain to look for opportunities, not threats.

4. Use Optimistic Self-Talk

Your words shape your world. Period. Use wording and phrasing that propels you into action. Negative self-talk creates hesitation. Positive self-talk builds courage.

Notice what happens to the way you feel, stand, and breathe when you read the following:

"I can't do it, it's too hard, I'm too dumb to do it, there is no way I can do it, and I'll look stupid in front of those people. They'll laugh at me, I'm just not cut out for this, I might as well just give up".

What happened inside your body? Did you notice your breathing got shallow, your head dipped, your brow furrowed?

Now notice what happens when you tell yourself the following: "I can do it, I'll find a way, it will work out no matter what, I'll get help from people when I need, I've done similar things before and worked it out, I've always got through it, I know I can get this done, I'm a problem solver, I've got this."

Did your body shift just now? Maybe you stood taller, breathed slower, or smiled a little?

There is a definite difference. That's the power of words in action. The words you consistently use in your day release chemicals in your body and shape your life experience. So when you engage in optimistic self-talk, you can instantly change how you think, how you feel, how you act, and how you live. When you change your words, you change your mindset. (More on supercharging your language in chapter 5).

5. Step Up and Do It

Action beats overthinking. Always.

When we consistently take action, we train our mindset to act before we stop for too long. It is the antidote for staying stuck in thinking things over and then finding a whole pile of reasons *NOT* to do something.

Take action and work it out on the way (remember, the *How* catches up!). That way, we are always moving. Moving closer, edging forward, creating momentum. We are taking action and moving towards our goals, objectives, and targets.

Say "Go" and go.

You've got about five seconds between thought and action before doubt sneaks in and drags you into analysis paralysis. Train yourself to decide and then *act*. Confidence comes from evidence, and the only way to collect evidence is to take the step. Take action.

You don't have to get it perfect, as this keeps you stuck in perfectionism or procrastination (see the Toxic Ten coming up next). Remember, *imperfect action is perfect* and is always the best action. Taking action provides the evidence and galvanizes our belief that we are a 'follow-through-er'.

Whatever it is you are working on, you just have to get it *going*. One tiny tweak. One small step forward. Just take action!

Mindset Isn't Magic – It's A Muscle.

Mindset is not magic, but it creates Magic. It's a method. A repeatable strategy that you *choose* to put into motion, especially when things get tough, uncertain, or unfamiliar. Mindset is like a muscle that you build, nourish, and look after. The *MINDSET RESET* Method is your go-to strategy to train your brain, fuel your emotions, and build an inner world so resilient that no external storm will shake it. This isn't just theory; it's a battle-tested strategy that Authentic Leaders, athletes, and world-changers use daily to rise, to lead, and to *thrive*.

So if you're waiting for certainty before you act - don't. Certainty comes *after* the leap. And the next level of your leadership is on the other side of doing it scared.

Fear the fear and do it anyway. Do it now.

You build confidence through repetition, focus, and courageous action. Do not wait for confidence to show up; you train it to show up. You decide you WILL have confidence. It is the result of taking action and building the evidence that you've got what it takes.

You don't hope for clarity, you *create* it. Create it by being committed to taking action, no matter what. When you lead with a mindset that serves you, you show up differently. You solve better, connect deeper, and perform stronger.

Your mindset is either your greatest limitation or your greatest liberation. The choice is always yours.

What Stops Us From Taking Action?

Agency is the mental toughness and decisive mindset to meet anything head-on, regardless of your past patterns or internal saboteurs. Many leaders we coach say things like, "Oh, but I'm a perfectionist," or "That's just because I'm a procrastinator."

One vital learning in leadership, as we've noted before, is that "What you say you are, you are." This isn't just a phrase we keep telling you. It's identity in action.

If you keep repeating the labels to yourself that do not serve you, you are reinforcing that identity. That is who you become. If a leader says, "I'm a tough leader, but fair." then they are. If another leader says, "I always find it hard to say 'no'," then they have become a people-pleaser.

No blame, shame, guilt, or judgment, just radical self-awareness.

Elizabeth

Let's introduce one of the most powerful frameworks I have encountered and use personally and professionally: *The Toxic Ten*. Developed by Joseph McClendon III,[20] refers to the 10 internal saboteurs that stop us from taking action and exercising agency across all areas of life.

The Toxic Ten:

1. **Procrastination**
   Delaying action due to fear, doubt, or lack of clarity, which fuels anxiety and stress.

2. **Hesitation**
   Pausing or delaying decisions because of fear or self-doubt, keeping you stuck in inaction.

3. **Fear of Failure**
   Avoiding action or risk due to the belief that making mistakes diminishes or defines your worth.

4. **Fear of Success**
   Resisting progress due to unconscious fears of responsibility, visibility, or not being worthy.

---

[20] Defeat The Toxic Ten with Joseph McClendon III. SR Blog [Internet]. 2024 Dec 11 [cited 2025 Nov 07].
   Available from: https://sr-blog.zohosites.com.au/blog/post/the-toxic-10

5. **Self-Doubt**

Questioning your own value, abilities, or decisions, undermining your confidence.

6. **Self-Loathing**

Harbouring deep shame or unworthiness that sabotages your self-image and potential.

7. **Impostor Syndrome**

Feeling like a fraud despite evidence of success, fearing you'll be exposed or 'found out'.

8. **Stress**

A mental and physical overload response to pressure that strains your body and mind.

9. **Overwhelm**

Feeling crushed by demands and responsibilities, leaving you mentally and emotionally drained.

10. **Fear of Rejection**

Avoiding visibility and vulnerability to protect against disapproval and loss of acceptance.

These patterns all have one common thread: **a feeling of unworthiness**.[21]

You Are Worthy!

You cannot lead Authentically if you believe you're not worthy of being your true self. If you're trying to be accepted or approved of by others, you're giving away your power. Worthiness doesn't come from them out there approving of things you do. Worthiness comes from within.

---

[21] Joseph McClendon III. Defeat The Toxic Ten. SR Blog [Internet]. 2024 Dec 11 [cited 2025 Nov 07].
Available from: https://sr-blog.zohosites.com.au/blog/post/the-toxic-10

"I say when I am worthy." No one else. It's not their business, *it's yours.*

The odds of you being born have been stated as more than 1 in 4 trillion. Let that land. The probability of your biological mother and father meeting, connecting, and creating YOU - the magnificent, unique, incredible being that you are - is astronomical. And if conception was difficult for your parents? You are even more miraculous.

Christine often reflects on this as she often says her parents tried for 15 years for her to be born. This presents even lower, more powerful odds of perhaps even 1 in 12 or 15 trillion. And yet, here she is. And here *you* are.

You are worthy. Own it. Declare it. Embody it.

Remember to say it *and* believe it through the techniques we share in this book, and step into your leadership role. Not with arrogance or ego, but with certainty, courage, and confidence. You are here for a reason. You get to lead, grow, and evolve.

Don't let the Toxic Ten steal that from you.

These saboteurs are learned patterns. They once kept you safe, but now they are keeping you stuck. If we ignore the patterns and default to the thinking that; *This is just how I am,* or *I've always been like that,* then we are reaffirming and holding onto the limiting pattern, which then creates a self-fulfilling prophecy.

Recognizing and noticing these patterns is your first power move, because: *What you say you are, you are.*

The way you think and speak either traps you in the Toxic Ten or frees you to take courageous action. In the next chapter, we explore how to supercharge your language and self-talk, because Authentic Leaders master their internal dialogue.

Taking Action 'Traps'

Many leaders get stuck in the loop of, "I just need to do a little more research/thinking on that before I act." This is often a disguised form of procrastination or fear. Ask yourself, What's really behind the delay? Is it fear of getting it wrong? Fear of being seen? Or the fear of what happens if I succeed?

Effective Leaders take *immediate* action.

This doesn't mean you jump blindly into high-risk actions without performing due diligence, it means making informed decisions quickly, checking in: "Is the Toxic Ten running the show right now or am I?" If you want a shortcut decision-making tool, head to Chapter 6 – *The Authentic Leadership Toolkit,* and come back here for more gems.

Those who take action despite resistance are the courageous ones who have embraced Agency. They live the mantra: **Think – Feel – Do – Have**. They step outside their comfort zone, on purpose. They master the ability to *go*.

The Courageous Mindset

What are the thoughts of these courageous leaders who take consistent action? These people believe that they *are* resourceful, that they *have* what it takes. That they will always find a way, no matter what. We explore more on this in Chapter 5 as well.

Authentic Leaders don't wait for conditions to be perfect before they act. They believe:

- "I am resourceful."
- "I'll always find a way."
- "I have what it takes."

And then take action with accountability, certainty, and courage. Knowing they have what it takes to deal with anything that comes next.

Christine is one of those people who demonstrates the power of agency on a daily basis. She takes brave, consistent, audacious action, no matter what. She chooses a constant state of resourcefulness, no matter what potential obstacles, resistance, or challenges arise. She embraces each situation with curiosity, fun, openness, innovation, and adventure.

Whether facing loss or grief, being passed over for team selection in her sporting career, experiencing workplace bullying, receiving a cancer diagnosis and treatment, stepping into a boardroom, or dealing with financial challenges. She uses every moment as fuel for growth, applying this to all her work and life, whether it's with multi-millionaire company owners, elite athletes, individuals, teams, or friends. That's the power of Agency.

Agency means: **no ifs, no buts, just action**.

If you hear yourself say, *"I can't do that, it's outside our remit,"* yet you *know* it is the right thing to do for your team or organization, then pause. Ask yourself: Is it really a structural barrier? What is behind this hesitation? Is it one of the Toxic Ten whispering in my ear?

If you end every day feeling exhausted, drained, and unable to switch off from work, which Toxic Ten is running the show? The overwhelm pattern. It may have helped you survive in the past, but they are no longer serving you or setting you up to *lead*!

Breaking Free From The Toxic Ten

The Toxic Ten are mental traps that create loops of fear, doubt, and inaction. Noticing and naming them is your first act of liberation.

You don't need perfection, you need persistence.

The key to overcoming the Toxic Ten is not perfection; it's persistence. Small, consistent changes in your mindset and habits which lead to transformative results over time. Start today by choosing ONE ACTION you've been avoiding, and implement! That single step can be the beginning of a complete identity shift. You're rewiring your brain in a different way. The more you act, the easier it gets.

Elizabeth

I used to think that everything had to be just so. A certain way of presenting self, a certain level of information, and a certain method for doing things. I didn't use the word "perfect" as I never thought of myself as a perfectionist; however, my actions were those of one.

I used to not take action, thinking I: *Can't post on social media until... Can't apply for this job because... Can't lead the team yet because...*

I wrapped my identity around this limiting pattern until I crashed and burned. I didn't recognize that every time I took a tiny step forward, I would create momentum like a wheel rolling downhill that gets faster and faster. Instead, I was stuck in my patterns without even noticing.

Remember this: Your responses are *just patterns.* They were created by your experiences throughout life to keep you safe and get you to where you are now. They are not permanent. They were created to help you, and now, you get to upgrade them. You get to choose *new patterns* that serve you more, empower you fully, and ignite your next level of leadership.

Celebrate these changes. Celebrate being YOU! *You now get to choose* to change the patterns of the past to new ones that serve you and set you up to create what you want to achieve. You get to choose to step into your next level of magnificence to lead yourself and others with authenticity! Without hesitation, without the overwhelm, without the fear!

Five Steps To Bust Through The Barriers

Here are five steps you can take to bust through the Toxic Ten, break free of past patterns, and create a more empowering way to lead.

Step 1: Become Self-Aware: Recognize and acknowledge your patterns of thinking and behavior. Notice your patterns. Name them. Understand how they served you - and how they now limit you. This awareness is the first step to change.

Step 2: Supercharge Your Self-Talk: Your language is either building your future or sabotaging it. Choose language that supports you and self-talk to rewire your brain. Replace negative thoughts with empowering ones. This will help you build resilience and internal drive (refer chapter 5).

Step 3: Embrace Discomfort: When the niggle shows up, it's an invitation to grow. Act *because* it feels unfamiliar, not in spite of it. Step outside your comfort zone and take action despite the fear and uncertainty. Authentic leaders embrace discomfort as a part of growth and development.

Step 4: Cultivate a Growth Mindset: Believe in your ability to learn and grow. Challenges are your classroom. View all challenges as *opportunities.* You get to develop new skills, new patterns, and greater knowledge. This mindset will help you persist in the face of anything that shows up.

Step 5: Build a Supportive Network: Surround yourself with Authentic Leaders who support and encourage you. Seek out mentors, coaches, and peers who expand your thinking, call you forward, and celebrate your evolution.

The STOP Technique: Reprogramming In The Moment

A powerful technique to use when you notice these thoughts and feelings showing up, is the STOP Technique. One of the quickest ways to break free from the grip of the *Toxic Ten*, to interrupt your state and rewire your brain in the moment. Joseph McLendon III calls this the **STOP Technique**, and it's a powerful neuro-encoding tool that helps you shift from being stuck in unresourceful emotions into a state of optimism and resourcefulness, fast.

We use it, we teach it, and we know it works!

Do this three times in a row and notice the change in mindset, and feeling. Put this into consistent daily action, and repeat this process, three times a day for 10 days. You will notice that you are stopping the default pattern of feeling and being limited by the Toxic Ten, and you are beginning to rewire the resourceful, empowered side of your brain.

Here is the four step process to follow:

1. **Feel 'bad' on purpose**
    First, lean into the "bad" feeling you're experiencing, whether it's doubt, frustration, comparison, or criticism. Notice it fully for a few seconds so you can identify it, feel it.

2. **Interrupt the pattern**
    Then, break the cycle. Say "STOP!" out loud, quickly stand up and shake your body. This jolts you out of that negative loop (changes your physiology, which changes your state).

3. **Feel 'good' on purpose**
    Now, deliberately shift into a powerful state. Put a big smile on your face (this releases oxytocin, endorphins and serotonin. Then recall a moment of joy, gratitude, or achievement. Move your body with energy, and embody that feeling. This is where your brain begins re-encoding the *new* pattern.

4. **Praise yourself**
    Anchor this new pattern by acknowledging the shift. Squeeze your fist and say "Yes!" or simply give yourself credit for choosing differently. This reinforces the new neural pathway and makes it easier next time.

With practice, this takes less than three minutes and retrains your brain to default toward optimism and resilience. Instead of being hijacked by the *Toxic Ten*, you reclaim control, rewire your state, and show up as the best, most resourceful version of yourself.

Leading With Authenticity

What does leading authentically mean?

- Taking fast, aligned action
- Making decisions with clarity and confidence
- Letting go of outdated patterns that no longer serve you
- Building the life and leadership style that YOU choose

Elizabeth

As Tony Robbins says, "When I say go, we go."

I fully embraced this last year when I decided to follow Christine's lead and plunge into ice baths five mornings a week. I personally hate the cold, hate being in the rain, wind, darkness, or doing crazy things. But I saw this challenge as a training ground. A way to practice doing hard things, create mental toughness, and practise the ability to *go*.

I have trained myself to embrace agency at the next level. "When I say go, we go". I go into the icy water, regardless of the weather, what happened the night before, or what I feel like when I woke up. I breathe out, and plunge. I trained my brain to take action regardless of how I *felt* or what the outcome would be.

Because I have trained this skill of 'I go', I now connect more deeply with people, make quicker business decisions, do things without hesitation, speak up for myself, and take brave action, even when it's uncomfortable. I embrace agency, not allowing the Toxic Ten to stop me from stepping into my ability to be authentic.

That's the power of Agency. That's the practice of Authentic Leadership.

Awareness brings change.

When you shine a light in the shadows, the shadow disappears. By following these steps and engaging fully with this playbook, you can break free from the past limitations, bust through the barriers of the toxic patterns, and step into your most courageous, confident, and authentic self.

We've loved writing this chapter for you, and it has shown you that Authentic Leadership doesn't start with position, privilege, or perfection; it starts with *mindset*. A courageous one. One that says: "I get to choose how I show up, no matter what."

You now have the tools: the MINDSET RESET method, awareness of the Toxic Ten, and a clear path forward, but the true transformation comes when you *use* them. Agency means owning your next step, even when it's uncomfortable. Especially when it is. You don't need to be fearless; you just need to move!

That's how you build the muscle. That's how you lead.

So when the voice of doubt creeps in, when perfectionism whispers, or the fear of judgment knocks at the door, pause and ask: *Is this my power speaking, or an old pattern playing out?* Then *answer with action*. Small, deliberate, consistent action. Declare who you are through what you do. Say it: **I am courageous. I am worthy. I am the leader of my own life.** Now prove it, one bold step at a time. The next level of your leadership isn't waiting for you, it's waiting **on** you. Let's go.

Want Permanent Results?

Christine and I can personally guide you through a neuroscience-based strategy that helps rewire your brain and release the grip of the Toxic Ten - permanently. It takes about 30 minutes. If you're ready to commit and are fed up with the Toxic Ten running the show, contact us https://waltinstitute.com/.

The following techniques throughout this book work brilliantly too; they may just take a little longer to embed when you do it on your own. Either way, *take action*. Lead from where you are now and shift your leadership with growth and expansion, one tiny tweak at a time!

Chapter Takeaways:

Agency Beats Intention – Action, not knowledge, creates change. Courage grows through movement, one step at a time.

All and Nothing - How you do *one* thing, is how you do *everything.*

Do It Scared – Courage isn't the absence of fear; it's taking action in spite of it. You build confidence through repetition, focus, and courageous action.

Tiny Tweaks, Big Momentum – Small, consistent actions compound into transformation over time.

Mindset is a Muscle – Train it daily through awareness, repetition, and reflection. Strength comes from consistent use.

Name the Toxic Ten – Identify and disarm your inner saboteurs to reclaim power and clarity.

Optimistic Language – The words you choose shape your chemistry, confidence, and courage.

Five-Second Rule – Decide and act before self-doubt takes hold. Momentum breaks through the fear.

Perfection Kills Progress – Waiting for perfection keeps you stuck. Imperfect action is perfect, and moves you forward.

Leading Forward:

What's your one key takeaway from the chapter (of course there will be more), that you are going to take action on NOW?

CHAPTER 5

From Words To Wisdom: Harnessing The Supercharged Language Of Leadership

"Words hold power. The power to inspire or intimidate, strengthen or weaken, expand or constrict. Choose them wisely."
—Elizabeth Pritchard

Ever been in a meeting when someone says something to you that is seemingly harmless, yet your inner dialogue kicks into overdrive?

"What did they mean by that? Are they saying I didn't do a good job? Damnit, I should have circled back and contacted that person, but I put it off. Now everything is going wrong, and it's all my fault. What an idiot. I always do this. I'm so useless."

Sound familiar?

This rhetoric used to be my norm until I learned the profound impact words have, not just those we speak aloud, but the ones we whisper inside our own heads.

Christine often asks people this simple yet revealing question: "Would you say that to your best friend?" The answer is ALWAYS no, and the follow-up is even more powerful: "Then why do you say it to yourself?"

If you are serious about stepping into your Authentic Leadership, one of the most important skills you can develop is noticing the language you use with yourself and with others.

We all know that words hold energy and are incredibly powerful. Just look at the work of Dr. Masaru Emoto, the Japanese researcher, known for his experiments on how words and emotions affect water molecules. In his book, *The Hidden Messages in Water* (2004), Emoto documented how positive words like "love" and "gratitude", when spoken to or written on the containers, changed the chemical structure of the molecules and created beautifully formed water crystals. In contrast, when the same water was exposed to negative words like "hate," "anger," or "fear," the resulting formations were fragmented, distorted, and chaotic. The vibration of the words literally changed the structure of the water.[22]

Think about this: Your body is composed of between 60-75% water.

What impact do your words, thoughts, self-talk, and communication have on you first, and then on everyone around you?

When you repeatedly tell yourself you are useless, a failure, or not good enough, you are not just indulging in harmless negativity, you're bombarding your cells with toxic energy.

That energy doesn't stay contained. It leaks. It spills out into your leadership, your conversations, your decisions, and your relationships. If you're someone who needs more *proof* of this impact, we've got an exercise for you coming up.

Feel It To Shift It: The Hidden Power Of Self-Talk

Pause for a moment. Tune in. What's the soundtrack playing in your mind today?

Whether we realize it or not, every word we speak to ourselves is sculpting the way we show up in the world. Tell yourself you're not good enough, that you're failing as a leader, that you're falling behind, and you will feel your shoulders round forward, your breath shorten, and your head bow. Your energy drops. Your posture slumps. The room feels heavier. It's like your entire nervous system gets the message: *Retreat. Collapse. Dim your light.*

---

[22] Emoto M. The hidden messages in water. Thayne DA, translator. Hillsboro (OR): Beyond Words Publishing; 2004.

People sense it, even if you haven't said a word out loud.

This isn't just a mindset; it's physiology. Your body listens to every word you say. When your self-talk is filled with doubt, criticism, and defeat, your physicality shifts to match that vibration. It drags your leadership presence down into the mud.

But here's the shift.

Speak to yourself like you would talk to the most brilliant, brave, powerful leader you admire.

Say: "I've got this. I'm learning. I'm showing up. I'm leading with heart."

Feel how everything changes. Your spine lengthens. Your chest expands. Your eyes lift. Energy returns to your voice. You become magnetic. Optimism, like a flame, reignites from within, and it's contagious.

We are not just thinking creatures. We are feeling, moving, expressive beings. The words we use to shape our internal dialogue directly shape our external impact. And Authentic Leadership begins right there, in the raw, unfiltered whispers we tell ourselves in the quiet moments.

Let's Get Real

As we have already covered, just *thinking positive* or chanting affirmations like a mantra on repeat isn't enough. You can't slap a smiley face over struggle and expect transformation. Repeating positive affirmations alone does not work if they're not anchored in with belief, emotion, and aligned action.

Neuroscience backs this up. In fact, affirming, empowering words activate the prefrontal cortex and spark motivation. But, if underneath those words there's doubt, fear, or unresolved stress, your brain defaults back to survival mode. The amygdala lights up. Cortisol spikes. Your body doesn't lie.[23]

---

[23] Fredrickson BL. The role of positive emotions in positive psychology: the broaden-and-build theory of positive emotions. Am Psychol. 2001;56(3):218–26.

The key is not just in what you say, it's in how deeply you *feel it, embody it,* and *live it.* Authentic Leadership demands that we go beyond surface-level positivity and develop self-talk that's embedded in truth, resilience, and a willingness to rise up, even when it's messy.

Words go deeper than just brain chemistry. Research by Dr. Bruce Lipton reveals that our thoughts, beliefs, and feelings don't just shape how we perceive the world; they directly impact how our *genes* function. In *The Biology of Belief* (2005), Lipton explains that our internal state - our dominant thoughts, emotional responses, and underlying beliefs - sends chemical signals throughout the body that can literally switch genes on or off.[24] Let that sink in for a moment. Your mindset has the power to influence your biology at a cellular level. You are not a passive victim of your genetic code; you are an active participant in your own evolution.

When you chronically think disempowering thoughts like *"I'm not good enough,"* or *"I'm a poor leader,"* or *"I'll never figure this out,"* you create an internal environment of stress, fear, and contraction. Your body then responds in kind: inflammation rises, immune response weakens, energy drops, and over time, your physical health pays the price.

But when you shift your inner dialogue to one of possibility, purpose, and self-compassion, you don't just feel better, you *function* better. Cells respond. Systems recalibrate. You become more resilient, not just mentally, but physically and emotionally.

This is the real power of language in Authentic Leadership: Owning the truth that the way you think and speak to yourself doesn't just influence your mood or motivation, but is actively sculpting your biology, shaping your leadership presence, and setting the emotional tone for everyone around you.

---

[24] Lipton BH. *The Biology of Belief: Unleashing the Power of Consciousness, Matter & Miracles.* Carlsbad, CA: Hay House; 2005.

If we are **thinking** one thing (a positive statement e.g. *I can do this*) and our body is still **feeling** the stress, doubt or past patterns of negative thought *(I cannot do this, I have never been able to do this, or I don't think I can)*, then there is incongruence between our mind and our body.

When there is incongruence between our mind and our body, our body will win! Hence, the meltdown will still happen, the crumbling will occur, and the self-doubt will take over.[25]

Dr. Joe Dispenza talks about the importance of alignment between our mind (our thoughts) and our body (our feelings and beliefs). He explains *congruence* as "a scientifically proven state in which mind and body are in alignment." In *Breaking the Habit of Being Yourself*, he explains how repeating the same thoughts and emotions rewires our brain, shaping our habits, for better or worse.[26]

We also know from Black and Slavich's research that living with chronic stress, especially stress triggered by negative self-talk, weakens our immune system and increases inflammation in the body.[27] This shows how much power our inner voice really has. It affects not just how we feel emotionally, but also our physical health.

For leaders, this is powerful stuff.

The words we say to ourselves, whether encouraging or critical, affect how our brain and body respond. When we catch ourselves thinking things like *"I failed again"* or *"I'm not good enough,"* it triggers stress hormones that make us feel anxious and tense. If this pattern of thinking

---

[25] Schwartz JM, Begley S. *The Mind and the Brain: Neuroplasticity and the Power of Mental Force.* New York: HarperCollins; 2002.

[26] Dispenza J. *Breaking the Habit of Being Yourself: How to Lose Your Mind and Create a New One.* Carlsbad, CA: Hay House; 2012.

[27] Black DS, Slavich GM. Mindfulness meditation and the immune system: A systematic review of randomized controlled trials. Ann N Y Acad Sci. 2016;1373(1):13–24.

occurs often, it can wear us down physically and emotionally, making it harder to show up fully as a true, powerful Authentic Leader.

When we choose words and beliefs that powerfully impact us and connect with positive statements at a deep, heartfelt level, something remarkable happens. This alignment between what we think, feel, and believe creates a state Dr. Dispenza calls "brain and heart coherence." It's like the brain and heart are working *together* in harmony, opening the door for real change and growth.

Authentic Leadership doesn't begin at the boardroom table, it begins within. It's not just about what you say or do outwardly; it's how you think, feel, and what you believe when no one else is watching.

Your inner dialogue, your self-talk, is the foundation. The words you speak to yourself shape your biology, your energy, and your ability to lead with presence and authenticity. When your self-talk is aligned with belief and emotion, when you truly *feel* the truth of your own worth, you create coherence between the mind and body. From this space, resilience strengthens, clarity sharpens, and genuine connection becomes possible.

This is more than a mindset; it's science. Lipton's research shows that your thoughts influence your gene expression. Dispenza demonstrates how emotional patterns shape your neurology. Black and Slavich prove how self-talk and stress impact your immune system. The evidence is clear: When we change the internal script, we don't just lead better, we live better.

That's the supercharged language of Authentic Leadership.

It's 'I', Not 'You'.

The first place to start supercharging your language (remember, this is self-talk and the spoken word) is to take ownership of your statements and your experiences with "I", not "You".

Consider the impact and difference of saying this to someone: *"You know when you go into a meeting and you're worried about whether you will say the right thing..."*

Stop. This is YOUR experience, own it for YOURSELF, don't project this onto someone else.

If you are talking with a team member or another person, and they are thinking, *No, I don't have that experience,* then you have just instantly created a communication break. They will be stuck back in that part of the statement, and you have just lost them. They will not be present with you in the conversation.

They will now probably be *thinking, No that's not me, so why are you saying I do that? Is there something behind that? What else are you trying to say?*

When you own your statement, you own your truth. You are stepping into your Authentic Leadership of self, first! Replace your statement with: *"When I go into meetings, I often worry whether I will say the right thing, and then I often keep quiet because I don't want to say something wrong."* Your understanding of self shows great awareness, and remember, awareness is the precursor to change!

Don't Use "But", Use "And"

This might seem like a small tweak in language, but it holds extraordinary power in shaping how you lead, influence, and connect. The word "but" is one of the most common ways people unintentionally erode trust, diminish confidence, and shut down open communication, without even realizing it.

Look at this example:

*"You did a really great job getting that client on board for the project, **but** let's make sure it's within the timelines next time."*

Now compare it to this:

*"You did a really great job getting that client on board for the project, **and** let's make sure it's within the timelines next time."*

How does each version make you feel?

When you say "but," you're not just adding another thought; you're erasing or discounting everything that came before it. Psychologically, the person only hears what follows the "but". Their brain translates it like this: *Forget the good part. Here's what you really need to fix.*

The word "and", on the other hand, is expansive. It builds. It holds space for both acknowledgment and opportunity. It allows you to celebrate success while also encouraging growth.

But divides. *And* connects.

Another Example:

*"It was great having your support for the project, **but** I think we need to relook at the processes that let us down."*

Versus:

*"It was great having your support for the project, **and** I think we need to relook at the processes that let us down."*

Notice the difference? The second version honors both the contribution *and* the opportunity for improvement. Nothing is negated. Nothing is dismissed.

Authentic Leaders use language intentionally. They understand that even the smallest word choice shapes trust, motivation, and collaboration.

And keeps people open. *But* shuts people down.

Remember:
- Start listening to yourself.
- Start noticing.
- Start switching.

Using your language intentionally is not soft. It's leadership.

Supercharge Your Language Self-assessment

When we *pause*, truly pause, and become aware of the words we speak to ourselves and others, we unlock the first door to transformation. This is not just self-help fluff; it's the neurochemical blueprint of change.

The moment we bring courage into that pause and consciously, purposefully, *intentionally* choose a different word, a different phrase, or a different internal truth, we trigger an entirely new cascade of emotions and biochemistry. Language is not passive; it's generative. It shapes how we feel, how we move, and how we lead.

> *"As I think, so I feel. As I feel, so I do. As I do, so I have."*
> *—Joseph McClendon III*[28]

This sequence isn't just poetic, it's powerful. If we want to shift how we lead in the boardroom, in the office, and in our teams, it begins long before the action. It starts in the invisible space between thought and word. That's where true Authentic Leadership is born. That's where behavior is shaped. That's where we begin to rewire old patterns and create new, powerful ways of *BEing*.

Want to lead with more impact? Speak with more clarity? Build deeper trust?

Then start by upgrading the language you use with yourself. When you change your words, you change your chemistry, and when you change your chemistry, you change your capacity.

---

[28] McClendon JM III. About – The Neuroencoding Institute. 2025 [cited 2025 Nov 21]. Available from: https://www.neuroencoding.com/about/

Statement *(no longer serving you)*	Sound Familiar? *Yes or No*	Change to...
No one ever listens to me.		Sometimes I feel unheard.
No one ever supports/helps me.		I am open to receiving support/help.
I shouldn't do that, I should know better.		I can do … /I do know …
I can't do that.		I am learning to master...
I'm so useless at …		I find this challenging/invigorating.
I'm always so exhausted.		My body is tired.
I'm never going to be able to do that.		Maybe I can learn how to do that.
I've always been like this.		My past pattern was...
Yes, I hear you, but...		I hear you, AND maybe I could find a way.
It will never work.		What is a way of being even more resourceful?
I don't want to be 'that' kind of leader.		I am choosing to be this kind of leader.
They don't do what I say.		What is a better way of communicating with the team/person to get follow through?
I'm time poor.		I always have enough time for the things I prioritise.
I'm just so busy.		I'm very productive today.
I'm always chasing my tail.		I get to pause for 10 seconds between each task.
No one understands what I have to deal with.		I have people who support me.
I'll never make it.		What can I put in place to meet this deadline?
They're better than me.		We all have our areas of genius.

Statement (*no longer serving you*)	Sound Familiar? *Yes or No*	Change to...
I always mess up.		I am doing the best I can with what I have!
I've failed again.		This didn't go as expected. What could I learn from this?
I'm such a loser.		Sometimes I am hard on myself, and I get to choose to ease up.
Everything's fine, don't worry about me.		What could I be missing here?
No one will like me.		I have the courage to be me.
I'm never good enough.		I am always enough – I do not have to 'do' anything to prove this.
I feel like an imposter.		Sometimes doubt creeps in when things are unfamiliar.
I don't trust myself.		I am learning to trust myself even more.
I don't want to let this go.		I am choosing to let this go.
I might not succeed.		Whatever the outcome, I will always learn something amazing.
What if it goes wrong?		What if it turns out okay?
I'm just so overwhelmed all the time.		I'm choosing to respond with clarity and calm.
It always takes a long time.		I'm exactly where I need to be, and every moment is part of my mastery.
It's always so hard.		It's unfamiliar, and I'm working through it.
I can't get this wrong.		Let's get this going in the right direction.
But it has to be perfect.		Maybe, imperfect action is just real progress.
I can't be bothered.		I am choosing to ease up.
I'm not clever enough.		I have amazing skills to do what I need to.

Statement (*no longer serving you*)	Sound Familiar? *Yes or No*	Change to...
I'm too old/young for this.		I'm in the perfect place to bring my skills.
I'm too...		I am enough, right here, right now.
But I have to do that.		I choose to...
I always struggle with that.		This is something I'm learning to navigate with more ease
I don't like conflict.		Conversation brings clarity.
I can't say no.		I get to identify what is right for me in this moment.

In putting this list together, both Christine and I found it really difficult to say all these phrases on the left that no longer serve us. We both felt heavy in the chest, anxious, disturbed, stressed, and had to open the window to let the negative energy out, move our bodies, and reaffirm the reframed good stuff.

This list has been collated from the people we work with and some of the things we used to say to ourselves. We have recognised the impact of the words and statements, and now choose to supercharge our own language and that which we speak to others. The impact is huge!

Remember - *whatever you focus on, you get more of.*

Every thought, every word, every phrase you repeat to yourself is either a deposit into your greatness or a withdrawal from your potential.

When we say things like, "I'm not good at this," or "I'll never get it right," or "I'm such a failure," we're not just expressing frustration; we're wiring our brain to believe it. Thought by thought, word by word, we carve neural pathways that become the roadmap of our reality.

Over time, these statements solidify into embedded beliefs. They start to shape how we see the world and ourselves. We unconsciously begin scanning for proof to validate our self-doubts, our limitations, and our stuck-ness.

And guess what? We find it, because that's what the brain does: It confirms the story we feed it.

This is how a self-fulfilling prophecy is born. The more we say it, the more we believe it. The more we believe it, the more it becomes our reality. Authentic Leadership built on these un-serving internal narratives becomes reactive, cautious, and disconnected not just from others, but from our own truth, creativity, and power.

But here's the moment everything can change.

When we pause to *observe* the words we say to ourselves, when we *bring courage* into that space and choose to speak differently, *we change everything.* We create a new chemical cascade, a new emotional response, and a new behavioral pathway. That's not fluffy theory, that's biology, neuroscience, and psychology in action.

If you want to change your leadership, your relationships, your performance, it doesn't start with strategy or structure. It starts in the invisible space between thought and language. It starts with one bold choice to speak differently.

Supercharge your language. Choose words that declare who you *are becoming*, not the doubts you're dragging behind. Speak with intention. Act with belief. Lead with power.

Authentic Leadership doesn't begin on the outside; it starts *inside* with the clarity of thought, the alignment of emotion, and the courage to speak truth into being. You are not here to repeat the past. You are here to *re-code* your future, lead with authenticity, and rise again and again as the empowered version of you that the world so desperately needs.

Say it. Believe it. Live it.

This is the new leadership story, and *you* are the author.

Chapter Takeaways:

Words Shape Reality – The language you use shapes your thoughts, emotions, and leadership presence.

Biology of Language – Words change brain chemistry, gene expression, and stress response. Choose your thoughts and words wisely.

Self-Talk Matters – How you speak to yourself sets the tone for your energy, confidence, and influence. If you wouldn't say it to a friend, don't say it to yourself.

Embodied Statements – Affirmations only work when they're felt, not just spoken. Head and heart congruence is essential to build solid optimism and belief.

Mind-Body Alignment – When thoughts, emotions, and actions align, authenticity flourishes.

Own Your Words – Use *I* instead of *you*. Take responsibility, own your statements, and strengthen your credibility.

Replace *But* with *And* – Expansive language builds collaboration and connection.

Pause Before Speaking – Conscious pauses allow wiser, more empowering communication formed from purposeful intention not reaction.

Reframe and Rewire – Choose empowering words to create more momentum and have better outcomes.

Authentic from the Inside Out – Speak with intention, act with belief, step into your power.

Leading Forward:

What's your one key takeaway from the chapter (of course there will be more), that you are going to take action on NOW?

CHAPTER 6

Your Authentic Leadership Toolkit

"You gain strength, courage, and confidence by every experience in which you really stop to look fear in the face. You must do the thing you think you cannot do." —Eleanor Roosevelt

This chapter invites you to explore the *practical tools, systems, and strategies* that help you lead with greater clarity, ease, and impact, through the lens of Authentic Leadership. These are the tools that allow you to create even more momentum, reduce stress, and build environments where people (including you) can truly thrive.

Your toolkit includes:

1. Calling things *as is* – as they truly are with clarity, care, and compassion
2. Setting and maintaining healthy, effective boundaries
3. Having courageous conversations
4. Running purposeful, empowering meetings
5. Creating agendas that inspire action and alignment
6. Using the present moment as your leadership anchor
7. Managing your time and energy with intention
8. The art of pre-framing and re-framing with influence and integrity
9. A simple decision-making strategy that works
10. How to actively celebrate progress and wins along the way

When we reflect on the tasks and conversations we lead each day, we're reminded of this: We always have a choice. A choice in our intentions. A choice in the language we use. A choice in how we show up every day.

It starts by asking yourself: Who am I BE-ing in this moment? Our doing then flows on from our being. The mindset we choose influences our behaviors, our words, and ultimately, our impact.

This chapter gives you practical tools to strengthen your leadership toolkit so you can lead with intention, clarity, and confidence. Let's approach this together with curiosity and a growth mindset, asking: *"What can I do even better?"* Because when we lead ourselves first, we are far better equipped to lead others with authenticity, courage, and care.

As you explore these tools and strategies, it's important to consider *how* you're applying them, not just to get more done, but to make a real difference. Information without action is useless! That's where the distinction between being *effective* and *efficient* becomes crucial.

Effective vs. Efficient: A Leadership Imperative

What's the real difference between being *efficient* and being *effective*?

Elizabeth

I used to take pride in being highly efficient. I was great at estimating how long things would take (including a generous buffer), ticking off to-do lists with precision, smashing through tasks, and impressing people with how much I could achieve in a single day.

But then something shifted. I realized that not everything I was doing was actually *effective*. Yes, I was achieving, but was I making a difference? Were the outcomes meaningful, lasting, and impactful?

Christine

I often describe it like this:

Efficiency is about speed and output. It's the mindset of just get it done, cut the corners, meet the deadline, tick the box. Efficiency often prioritizes tasks over people, and productivity over purpose. It can be about win/loss, black/white thinking, and choosing the fastest or cheapest route, often at the expense of quality or depth.

Effectiveness, on the other hand, is about meaningful progress. It's about learning, improving, and developing capability in ourselves and others. It takes the whole picture into account. It might take a little longer up front, but it lays a solid foundation that leads to better outcomes, stronger teams, and more sustainable impact.

Whichever view you relate with most, the real power comes from knowing the difference, and using both. When we pair efficiency with intention, we stop just doing and start truly leading.

The Cost Of Efficiency Without Effectiveness

A powerful (and tragic) example of this was the *Deepwater Horizon oil spill*. On April 20, 2010, the Deepwater Horizon drilling rig, operated by BP, suffered a catastrophic blowout in the Gulf of Mexico. The explosion killed 11 workers and led to the largest marine oil spill in history, releasing approximately 134 million gallons of oil over 87 days.

Investigations revealed that cost-cutting measures and a focus on expediency contributed to the disaster. Decisions were made to save time and money, such as using fewer centralizers during cementing operations, which compromised well integrity. Safety concerns raised by workers were overlooked or dismissed, and critical tests indicating problems were misinterpreted or ignored.

In his book *The Slow Fix*, Carl Honoré discusses how BP's approach exemplified the pitfalls of seeking quick solutions without addressing underlying issues. He notes that BP was slow to acknowledge the severity of the spill and reluctant to take full responsibility, highlighting a culture more attuned to immediate results than long-term accountability.[29]

---

[29] Honoré C. *The slow fix: Solve problems, work smarter, and live better in a world addicted to speed.* New York: HarperCollins; 2013.

The Role Of The Authentic Leader

As an Authentic Leader, you must learn to balance both. You're not just getting tasks done, you are developing people. You are building trust, capability, and connection. You're not just focused on the end goal; you are investing in how your team gets there, and who they become in the process.

Imagine bringing someone's strengths into a task and aligning that with the challenge at hand. That's when people hit what performance psychologists call *the performance zone* - the Yerkes-Dodson Law. You create just enough stretch to grow without overwhelming, and that's when people thrive.[30]

And when they *really* thrive, they enter *flow.* That incredible state was first described by Mihaly Csikszentmihalyi, where time disappears, focus deepens, and everything just clicks. In flow, you're not forcing or faking, you're aligned with your strengths, your purpose, or your "zone of genius." That's where true performance and fulfillment live.[31]

Elizabeth and I had the privilege of attending an intimate workshop with Csikszentmihalyi, which was amazing. Listening to him describe the state of being so fully immersed in a task, where time disappears and self-consciousness fades, resonated deeply.

It isn't just theory; it is a powerful reminder that the best leaders don't push people harder; they help them *align.* Align with their purpose, with their strengths, and with stretch. That's when we move from pressure to *presence,* and leadership becomes effortless, energizing, and effective.

---

[30] Yerkes RM, Dodson JD. The relation of strength of stimulus to rapidity of habit-formation. *J Comp Neurol Psychol.* 1908;18(5):459–82.

[31] Csikszentmihalyi M. *Flow: The psychology of optimal experience.* New York: Harper & Row; 1990.

What Kind Of Leader Will You Choose To Be?

Efficiency is important, but without effectiveness, it's empty.

Efficiency gets it done.

Effectiveness makes it count.

So, here's the challenge: How can you BE bold, BE intentional? Supercharge your Authentic Leadership by choosing effectiveness first and letting efficiency follow. Because when you combine meaningful impact with focused execution, you create leadership and teams that truly last.

1. Calling It As Is

If it's sh*t, it's sh*t. Don't sugarcoat it, and don't ignore or pretend it's not showing up as it is. When something flies in our face, recognize it for what it really is and call it *as is*.

Examples of this may include the contract you worked on for months, building the relationship with the client, nurturing it, answering their questions, working and reworking the proposal, and then at the last minute, they said a flat "NO."

In that first moment, what is your reaction?

If you jump into positive BS, then you are denying your response. You are pretending, and your cells and body will know it. You will create incongruence between your mind and body, and your body will realize it, resulting in a kickback.

Other examples could be when a child or partner is sick and you need to cancel a business trip. Or maybe you were applying for that promotion that you so deserved, and then found out you didn't get it. What about that time when you missed a plane because of an accident on the freeway, or didn't get to present what you wanted to because the CEO went overtime. Or that moment when, for the fourth time, you explained a process to someone and they still failed to meet the standard.

Anything and everything that happens in our lives becomes a moment when we can first recognize its immediate impact on us and call it *as is*. Allow yourself to have a *nano tanty* (a small tantrum), in a safe environment that does not impact others, of course.

Let yourself feel it, with openness, honesty, and rawness.

Elizabeth

The vital step is the one that comes next.

Remember Christine's experience of receiving a diagnosis? She reacted with truth, vulnerability, authenticity, and then… she *chose* to shift her focus and create the next step forward. I, too, have been learning over the past decade to shorten my reaction time. Many times, I would sit in the yuck, the situation, the negative emotion of it, replaying the event in my mind - talking about it, dreaming about it, and constantly thinking about it.

I remember the time I had a verbal contract for some work as a consultant. I met with the company, sent emails back and forth, received promises of a contract, and then, a week before I was supposed to start, I learned that they had contracted someone else into the role and didn't have the decency to tell me about it.

I was livid. I was raging. I was so angry that I even went outside, yelled loudly, and smashed something. I felt betrayed, furious, indignant, resentful, and disrespected. And then I turned on myself and decided I was not good enough, weak, worthless, and helpless.

In contrast, there are those times when I play down the effect, belittle the impact, and think, *Oh well, it's only a small thing and it will work out. I can find a way. It doesn't really matter.* In those moments, I was BS-ing myself, and my body and health suffered from this.

In the moments something unexpected shows up, we get to be real and face what has just happened first. Calling it *as is* is the first step in shifting from the reality of what has just happened, to then allow the space where we get to choose what comes next.

It's all about awareness and choice.

An example of this is when I get into an ice bath (at 10 degrees Celsius, 50 degrees Fahrenheit). For two days, I did the *let's pretend it's warm,* method when stepping in and going into the water. By doing that, I was experimenting with my mindset around what I thought, told myself, and focused on, so that I could build a stronger, tougher way of following through.

What I found was that my responses and the time it took for my body to settle in the cold took longer, was more uncomfortable, and felt like I was out of control. The next two days, I changed this and called it *as is.*

I stood by the side of the tub in preparation and went through the breathing ritual. Before stepping in, I stated, *it's cold and I step in easily -* and then I did! Remember, if there is incongruence between thought and body, then there is internal conflict, and it is much harder for us to follow through.

When I acknowledged reality as it truly was and called it *as-is* and set myself up to step in easily, then all of my brain, heart, emotions, and body were fully aligned with congruence.[32] They were able to work together, which allowed me to adapt to the external environment with ease and speed.

The time it takes between the *as is* and the next step is also within our hands. It is not determined by what *they* did to us, or what happened. We get to train ourselves on reducing the time we stay in our heightened emotions and then what we choose next. It is just a pattern and one highly effective tool we get to develop in our toolkit.

---

[32] Dispenza J. *You Are the Placebo: Making Your Mind Matter.* Carlsbad (CA): Hay House Inc.; 2014.

One way of shortening the time frame is to set a timer for 5 minutes. Allow yourself to feel your feels - anger, irritation, disappointment, betrayal, whatever it is. Allow yourself to say what you are thinking, unfiltered. Honor yourself and your emotions in that moment and open up to what is.

Then, when the timer goes off, this is your signal to choose again!

Choose a way forward, choose to supercharge your language, or choose a different focus. That way, you will move on, and not 'cling' onto the emotions that first came up, or choose to hang onto the suffering.

Here is the three-step RAP method we use to embrace the *as is* strategy.

- R – Recognize what is happening and your instant response to it
- A – Accept your feelings, thoughts, and emotions around the situation
- P – Permission, give yourself permission to feel the feels, and validate where you are at

Next time you are faced with something unexpected, go through the RAP method with honesty and openness. Then, YOU get to choose what comes next, and the speed at which you shift into resourcefulness in the leadership of yourself and others, in that moment.

And this is a wrap on the RAP!

Let's dive into the next tool in our toolkit: Boundary Setting.

2. Setting Effective Boundaries

"Boundaries are there to enhance, not to punish,"
—Christine Burns

When we approach the skill of boundary setting from the intention to enhance, embellish, and make things better, you will find that setting and keeping boundaries becomes easier to do.

Many people we work with say, "But I can't put myself first, that's selfish."

Roxana's Story

Take Roxana - a leader who was training with us to become an Authentic Leader. She was amazing at her job, recognized internationally for her skills in her field, and loved doing what she was doing, except for one thing - leading.

Her role title was Team Leader with 12 people in her team. She realized that she was always making time for them and neglecting her own needs for work time and space. She recognized that something had to change.

To her, boundaries were something other people did, but she could not. She'd tried in the past to set them, but felt guilty or found that over time they had disappeared. So, we began with exploring what she was telling herself about setting boundaries and we tackled them in small steps.

The first thing we worked on was something that she said bugged her the most: "Never getting solid time to do what I need to do, because people keep interrupting me." She held an open door policy because she wanted to be approachable, but this seemed to backfire. She was beginning to miss deadlines, and was often working in the evenings and weekends just to "get things done."

This is common for so many leaders we work with, and here is how we tackled it together.

We explored her beliefs around boundaries and what they meant to her. She identified that she really admired "X" as they seemed to have great boundaries in place, and it appeared to work for them. We began asking a host of questions so Roxana could consciously recognize her thoughts about boundaries.

- What does a boundary mean to you?
- What type of person sets a boundary?

- What does it mean to others when you say "No"?
- What is preventing you from saying, "Not at this moment, I can see you at that moment"?
- What if you saw a boundary as a way to enhance?

Ultimately, we wanted her to consider what it would take for her to reframe the meaning of *boundary* to include a way to enhance work outputs, communication, time management, fulfilment, and purpose.

"But," she would always say, "my team might not..." then always a pause. She knew what was behind this pattern. "They may not like me."

So, *this* is what was holding her back. Remember, no blame, shame, guilt, or judgment. When we notice what is happening and patterns that we are repeating, then we can turn it around.

With Roxana, our goal was to turn this pattern and belief around and have the courage to be disliked to set a great example for everyone on her team.

You can do this too. Take back control of YOUR diary. Take back control of YOUR obligations and outputs so that WE - being you, your team, and your organization - win!

An amazing book we have both read and listened to is *The Courage To Be Disliked* (Kishimi and Koga, 2013).[33] An incredible book that talks through the objections we may have as to why we think we cannot set boundaries.

Things like:

- I've never been able to
- It's just not me
- What if they don't like it/me?

---

[33] Kishimi I, Koga F. *The courage to be disliked: The Japanese phenomenon that shows you how to change your life and achieve real happiness.* New York: Atria Books; 2018.

- What if they think I'm pushy?

What if... what if...

Think about this: *What if* people see you modeling Authentic Leadership, setting boundaries in place at various times of the day, *and* you remain approachable and responsive to the requests and needs of the team? What if they admire the skill they see in you of setting effective boundaries and sticking to them?

When you first start setting boundaries, start small. You can say, "Between 10:00 a.m. and 12:00 p.m., I am available for meetings or drop-ins at these times *only*, as I'm focusing on my priorities for the day."

What is the message that this sends?

- I am important enough to prioritize.
- It is good practice to have solid times to focus and complete our priority tasks.
- When I show up being my best self and feel like I'm accomplishing what I need to in a day, we all win.

Ways To Implement This:

Put a note in your email signature - highlight when you *are available* (not when you are *not* available). Such as, "I am available for consultation between 8:30 a.m. and 10 a.m., and 2 p.m. and 4 p.m. each day. I will answer my emails at 8:00 a.m., 12:30 p.m. and 4:00 p.m."

Let staff know about your availability in your meetings and remember to tell them when you ARE available. Do not focus on the NOT. Let them know that from now on, things will be different.

These specific statements are based on Neuro-Linguistic Programming (NLP), which is based on the premise that the language we use influences how we think, feel, and behave. By intentionally shaping words and internal dialogue, individuals can reframe perceptions and create new neural pathways that reinforce desired beliefs and outcomes.[34]

The statement "I am" gives you permission to set something different in place. Of course, you also *get to* set up a safety net for any emergencies that may happen, and remember to ask yourself:*Is anyone going to die if I'm not consulted until after 12:00?*

Depending on your role and industry, you get to answer this question, and put parameters around these boundaries for your team. Determine up front when the rule or boundary could possibly be broken. Keep this tight, and YOU GET TO CHOOSE.

Next, you *get to* reinforce this. As with any new strategy put in place, there can be resistance to the change, be it thoughtlessness or simply a desire to buck the system. As an Authentic Leader, you get to choose to reinforce the parameter each time someone steps over it.

If they knock on the door, you can say, "Is this one of those times of high emergency we have talked about?" Tell them that a yes or no will suffice. If they answer with a no, then reinforce: "I will be available to deal with this at 12:00 p.m."

Another way of reinforcing the change in boundaries is putting a note on your door: *Available at 12:00 noon.* Remember, do not disturb. And simply return to your work. Don't engage in stories, listening, or time wasting. Simply reinforce the boundary and return to your work.

This takes practice, and usually within two to three times of restating this, people begin to respect the boundary in place and live with it productively.

---

[34] Cheal M. An investigation into how neuro-linguistic programming can be a source of positive psychology interventions to increase self-esteem and subjective well-being in psychologically healthy populations. In: *Current Research in NLP.* Vol 2. 2010.

This is not about being mean, this is about you stepping into your abilities to lead authentically. You get to reframe the language and supercharge the opportunity for the benefit of you, your team, and your organization.

3. Courageous Conversations

Many people label conversations as *tough*, *difficult*, or *hard*. But the words we choose shape our experience. If we frame a conversation as difficult, chances are it will feel exactly like that - difficult.

Language has power: What we focus on, we amplify.

What if, instead, we chose to call it what it truly is for an Authentic Leader: a Courageous Conversation? What would that do to our mindset, our physiology, our emotions, and our confidence?

When we change the language, we change the energy we bring, and ultimately, the outcome. Approaching a conversation through the lens of courage, clarity, and compassion sets a foundation built on reality, honesty, authenticity, and the desire to create a *win-win-win* - for ourselves, for the other person, and for the organization.

Here's where it gets even more powerful. When we choose to have courageous conversations, it's not about trying to control how others respond. It's about choosing to show up as *courageous*.

That shift in mindset changes everything. Instead of being driven by fear, worrying about others' reactions, or trying to manage every outcome, we focus on *who* we are being.

In that moment, you can tell yourself, "I get to be courageous. I get to speak with clarity and compassion." That's the part you can control - your energy, your intention, and your delivery. From that grounded place, the message lands stronger, and the connection runs deeper.

Preparation Matters

Courageous conversations require thoughtful preparation. Ask yourself:

- What is my true intention for this conversation?
- What outcome do I want to achieve?
- What will help put the other person at ease?
- How can I create space for them to share openly and feel heard?

As Authentic Leaders, we must hold ourselves accountable to these truths:

- We are equals as human beings, regardless of the titles we hold, we both hold value and have skills in different areas.
- We are both *doing the best we can with what we have* in this moment.
- While we may not always align, judgment, assumption, or unrealistic expectations will only derail the conversation and disconnect us from each other.

Ensure the other person knows ahead of time the general topic of the conversation and the expected outcome. This reduces anxiety and sets a clear, safe frame.

Prepare your opening statement with intention and care. Make it clear that you will bring openness, listen actively, and work together towards clarity on next steps.

For example:

"Thanks for meeting with me today to discuss how things are going with the project. Over the next 45 minutes, I'd like to share what I've observed about timelines not met, hear your perspective, and work together to shape a clear path forward."

Notice the tone: honest, authentic, open. There's no blame, no assumption, no hidden agenda, just clarity of purpose and the intention to listen and collaborate.

The Mindset Shift

Remember this truth: Every person is doing the best they can with what they know, even if that's not aligned with your standards or the organization's expectations. Your role is not to agree or to fix. Your role is to listen - *truly listen.* You don't have to like or agree with their perspective for it to matter. It is *their perspective.* In that moment, it is *their truth.* Your job is to respect that truth while staying anchored in your responsibility as a leader.

Courageous conversations are not about being right. They are about being real. They are about bringing humanity, clarity, and accountability into the room at the same time.

The PRISM Formula

Effective courageous conversations can be set up using the **PRISM Formula**. A prism refracts light and helps people see things differently. It is a way of gaining clarity and brings to light things that are hidden.

P – Prepare

- Set your clear intention: What's this conversation really about?
- Pre-frame the conversation with care and clarity.
- Focus on outcomes that serve people, purpose, and progress (win-win-win).

R – Respect

- Respect their time, energy, and perspective.
- Ensure psychological safety is at the forefront of your mind.
- Reflect on your role: Are you listening to understand, not to defend?

I – Invite

- Invite them with transparency about *why* this matters.

- Offer choice and dignity: Invite, don't demand.
- Make space for their voice. Set the tone of curiosity and care.

S – Speak Truth, Stay Open

- Speak clearly, calmly, and kindly - stay anchored in facts, not assumptions.
- Be open to surprise: your truth may not be the only truth here.
- Steer towards outcomes, not blame.

M – Move Forward Together

- Agree on what happens next.
- Clarify commitments or changes required.
- Reaffirm respect and appreciation, regardless of difficulty.

Using the PRISM method helps you set yourself up, set up the situation, and provides an optimal setting to hold the conversation. Remember, the other person's response is their responsibility, and beyond your control. However, as an Authentic Leader, you get to set yourself up, set the situation and environment up, and then go with the flow, with honesty, transparency, and integrity.

A Real Life Example Of The PRISM Formula In Action

Scenario:

A team member was consistently failing to follow through on agreed tasks, blaming others for her lack of progress, and avoiding conversations about accountability.

P- Prepare:

I spent 10 minutes getting clear on my intention: To hold a courageous conversation focused on understanding, accountability, and finding a constructive path forward. I noted my opening statement and the positive outcome I was aiming for.

R- Respect:

I considered her circumstances - knowing mornings were hectic with school drop-offs and that both of us were mentally fresher mid-morning, I scheduled the meeting thoughtfully for 10:30 a.m. This small step demonstrated care and respect for her well-being.

I - Invite:

I sent her a clear, respectful invitation:

"Let's meet to discuss the recent lapses in meeting timelines. This is a chance for us both to explore what's happening and work together on a way forward."

This invitation set expectations while signaling safety and collaboration.

S - Speak:

During the conversation, I stayed present and grounded in curiosity and objectivity. I used facts, not assumptions, and kept my emotions in check. I modeled *above the line* behaviors (see Chapter 9) to create psychological safety for her to do the same.

M - Move:

We talked about the next steps. I clearly stated the expectations of the company, and asked if she could meet these. We agreed on clear expectations, timelines, and checkpoints. I outlined the consequences of unmet expectations. Both of us took notes, and I followed up with a summary email to confirm our agreed actions.

Yes, emotions arose during the meeting for her: frustration, blame, and even tears. As an Authentic Leader, I validated her feelings without feeding into them. I asked open, compassionate questions that helped her move through the emotion towards clarity. We focused on what we could change, not what we couldn't.

Ultimately, it became clear her behaviors and values did not align with those of the organization, and we let her go. Although letting her go wasn't the outcome we initially hoped for, it was the right decision - for her happiness, and for the team's ability to move forward and thrive together.

The Takeaways:

This was a courageous conversation where we honored our values, kept egos in check, put judgment aside, and dialed up compassion and honesty. PRISM gave me the structure and confidence to lead the conversation well, even when the outcome was tough.

When used consistently, **PRISM is a life-changing tool for courageous conversations**. It works in professional and personal life alike. Whether it takes two minutes or two hours to prepare, the more you practice it, the faster and more natural it becomes. Courageous conversations demand courage - courage to reflect on yourself, your intentions, your words, and your actions.

If you want to lead yourself and others well, this is a non-negotiable skill to embrace and master.

4. Running Purposeful And Powerful Meetings

How many times have you sat in a meeting that followed this pattern:

- Started late - "We are waiting for __ to arrive."
- Spent half of the meeting talking through what has happened and getting reports from each department
- Spent the next chunk of time for the CEO or meeting lead to give you information about what is happening next (without any discussion)
- Had less than 5 minutes left for discussion around the most important thing on the agenda

Hundreds and hundreds of meetings are run like this, which is ineffective, and a waste of time and skill.

Ineffective meetings are one of the biggest hidden energy leaks inside organizations. They drain attention, motivation, creativity, and, ultimately, trust. Meetings consume valuable time, yet far too often, they achieve very little. This is not just poor practice, it is poor leadership.

Christine

I remember working in a place where we were lucky enough to have an entire hour carved out for lunch when everyone was available - a rare and valuable opportunity to collaborate. Yet, every time we had our staff meetings during this slot, it was a complete waste of time.

The first half of the meeting was always filled with rehashing old news, reporting on things that could have easily been shared via email, and endless chatter about issues that didn't matter. By the time we finally got to the key discussion points or critical decisions, there were barely 10 minutes left. People were already clock-watching or needing to get back to work, and nothing important ever got done. It was frustrating, disempowering, and a prime example of time misused and potential squandered.

Authentic Leadership recognizes that how we gather people - whether virtually or in person - reflects the culture we are cultivating. Meetings are never neutral. They either build clarity, connection, and momentum, or they diminish it.

We invite people into meetings to connect minds, solve problems, make decisions, and shape the future. Not to passively consume information or relive the past. When we honor people's time, we honor their contribution. When we waste it, we diminish their potential.

Every meeting represents a significant investment of collective energy. If you have 10 people in the room (or online) and the meeting is 60 minutes long, you have used 600 minutes of company time. That's 10 hours of time! Over one day of productivity, so you'd better make sure it is spent in a super effective *and* efficient manner.

Meetings are not just about exchanging information. Information can be shared in an email, a recorded video, or a brief update. Meetings exist to leverage the collective intelligence in the room, to think together, plan together, and solve together.

Authentic Leadership understands that time is precious; therefore, meetings are about creating shared clarity, not filling calendars.

When you approach meetings with intentionality, you create psychological safety. You set the tone that every voice matters, every moment counts, and everyone's contribution is valued. This is how trust is built, cultures are shaped, and momentum is maintained.

The Difference Between Attendance And Engagement

It's easy to confuse attendance with engagement. Just because people are in the room, or logged in, doesn't mean they are present. Being present comes from clarity of purpose, clear expectations, and a culture of respect.

A well-prepared meeting invites people to show up with focus, not to sit passively while information is downloaded. When people are clear on why they are there, how they can contribute, and what the meeting aims to achieve, engagement naturally increases.

Preparation is key. Circulate relevant reports, updates, and information in advance. Invite contributions to the agenda beforehand so people can prepare with intention. An agenda isn't simply a list of topics; it is a tool for creating focus, guiding energy, and shaping outcomes (see below).

Prioritize what matters most. Important discussions must be at the start of meetings, not the end. Decision-making requires fresh energy and clear thinking, not the leftovers of a long agenda.

The Ripple Effect Of Purposeful Meetings

How we run meetings says everything about how we lead. Meetings run with clarity, intention, and respect elevate trust, sharpen focus, and drive momentum. Meetings run out of habit erode morale, waste energy, and reinforce mediocrity.

Authentic Leadership is about choosing the former, every time. Not out of obligation, but because you recognize that where focus goes, energy flows.

When you craft meetings with precision, when you invite participation with care, when you hold time as sacred, you create environments where people thrive. And thriving people build thriving organizations.

Your leadership is seen in every choice you make, including how you choose to gather people, guide conversations, and close with clarity. Meetings are moments of leadership in action. Use them wisely.

Here's what you *can* do to run effective meetings:

- Select the RIGHT timeframe for the type of meeting (see more below)
- Have an effective agenda (coming up next)
- Start every meeting on time, regardless of who is in the room
- Open the meeting with a definite start
- Get all reports on PAST events sent through as pre-meeting papers BEFORE the meeting
- Set the expectation for ALL members of the team to do the pre-work and come prepared
- List the priority items up FIRST on the agenda
- Be prepared to ask individuals for their input if they are not contributing
- Close down the over-talkers with courage, kindness, and certainty
- Have a time keeper in every meeting (aligned with the agenda times)
- If additional things come up outside of the agenda, negotiate actions with the team (e.g., car park for next meeting, adjust today's agenda to fit it in, have a 1-1 meeting later)

- Every topic has a decision/action/person/date. Even if this is the final discussion on this topic, and no actions are required
- Finish the meeting on time, with a definite end

5. Agendas: Where Leadership Precision Meets Respect

There is a reason so many meetings fall flat before they even begin, and it starts with the agenda. Or more specifically, the absence of a purposeful, intentional agenda.

How many times have you received either no agenda (turning up not knowing what will be discussed), or an agenda that looks more like a shopping list:

Example:

- Project X timelines
- Professional development funding
- Work function
- What's next on the radar
- FYI

Agendas are *not* shopping lists of topics that the team has no idea about, are unclear about what is being focused on or what is required of them. Shopping lists offer no clarity on focus, no guidance on preparation, and no direction towards outcomes. This is not leadership in action; it is simply going through the motions.

Purposeful Agendas Create Purposeful Meetings

Every item on your agenda needs to answer these questions clearly:

- What specifically are we addressing?
- Why does this matter right now?
- What is the desired outcome - discussion, decision, or action?

- How much time are we allocating?
- Who is leading this conversation?

Agendas are not just for the meeting lead; they are for everyone in the room. This is why contributions to the agenda need to happen before it is finalized. When people have input into what's on the table, ownership increases, responsibility deepens, and engagement rises.

Send agendas at least five days prior to the meeting. This gives people time to prepare, read background papers, and gather insights. It creates space for informed contribution, not reactive conversation or passive apathy. Leadership is about creating environments where people can bring their best thinking, not where they are forced to think on the fly because of poor preparation.

Always prioritize the MOST important topics FIRST - do not leave them to the end.

If a conversation begins to stall, ask:

- Do we have the right people here to make this decision?
- Do we have all the information we need?

Stuck decisions aren't often about disagreement; they are usually about missing pieces. Name it, gather what's needed, and move forward with clarity.

Not everything belongs in a team meeting. Many updates can be shared through reports, emails, or short recordings. Meetings are not about recounting the past in detail or giving department reports. The past is done. Do not waste people's time and cognitive energy. The question that needs to be asked and brought to the meeting is: What have we learned, and how does that shape what happens next?

Other ways to explore the *past* are to ask: What are the red flags that need to be discussed and problems to solve? What are the mistakes that have been made that need to be opened up, discussed, and addressed?

When this is the focus of team meetings, you get to embrace the learnings and address the risks when they are small - without attributing blame, discussing openly, and mitigating to prevent further risk.

If there's no need for discussion or decision, there's no need for a meeting time. Respect people's time and attention by keeping meetings focused on what truly requires collective thought, conversation, and commitment.

Shared Responsibility – A Marker Of High Standards

At every meeting, every member of the team has a shared responsibility.

They have a responsibility to be on time, to do the pre-work, to be fully prepared, to contribute actively, and to be present (no poor behaviors of multi-tasking, answering emails, or checking phones).

Carefully consider who needs to be in the room. Inclusion is meaningful when people are there for a purpose. If someone has no contribution to make, their time is better spent elsewhere. If people have nothing to contribute to the items on the agenda, then why are you wasting their time and having them in the room?

When agendas are crafted with precision and purpose, meetings become spaces of progress, not frustration. They become a reflection of leadership that respects people's time, honors their contribution, and sets the tone for how work gets done.

Meetings that waste time diminish trust. Meetings that focus on time create momentum.

Where clarity leads, confidence follows. Where focus is sharpened, results improve. And where leadership is intentional, people thrive.

That is the power of a purposeful, powerful agenda.

Here is an example of an Effective AND Efficient Agenda:

WALT Institute Meeting Agenda - 20 August 20XX *(usually in a landscape format)*

Attendees:

Apologies:

Chair: HG   *Time Keeper: BK*

Item	Result required	Preparation required	Time and who is presenting	Actions (Completed at the meeting) What: Who: When by:
Welcome and connection	For the team to be present and connected.	NO	2 minutes Led by HG	
Project X timelines need renegotiating	Brief discussion to identify any gaps not already noted. Confirm timelines and responsibilities to meet the new KPIs.	YES, Read the KPI document. Bring any gaps/risks.	13 mins EP presenting	
Applications required for professional development funding	Process to be confirmed and shared. Please bring your #1 priority to the meeting to share.	YES, bring your top PD request.	7 minutes CB presenting	
Confirming 'work function' venue details	3 options sent around, brief discussion, and final decision to be made.	YES, rate the options *before* the meeting.	7 mins BK presenting	
Next on the radar For info – not for discussion	To be presented.	NO	2 minutes EP presenting	
Conclude – rate the meeting (each person scores the meeting with a brief comment – aiming to improve each time!)	Rate 1-5 and reason why for each person.	NO	4 minutes Led by HG	
Next meeting	**27 August 20XX 10:30 – 11:05 a.m.**			

As an Authentic Leader, you have the opportunity and the responsibility to model what effective, efficient, and purposeful agendas look like in action. Every agenda you craft signals to your team that their time matters, their contributions are valued, and their energy deserves to be focused where it counts.

This is how you build cultures of trust, accountability, and high performance, not through words alone, but through the way you lead every meeting, every conversation, every moment. Agendas are not administration; they are leadership in action.

6. Using The Present Moment As Your Leadership Anchor

One of the most powerful yet overlooked tools in Authentic Leadership is the ability to return - again and again - to the present moment. The present is where your influence, decisions, and leadership truly live. It's where clarity, connection, and calm action reside.

Anchoring yourself in the now allows you to lead with purpose, not from habit or fear. The present moment is your only true access point for creating change, building trust, and making aligned decisions.

Authentic Leadership asks us to honor the flow of time - to consciously dip into the past to gather learning, to glance to the future to check our direction, but always to bring ourselves back to the present to act. If we cling too tightly to the past, we risk becoming stuck in outdated narratives, regrets, and self-limiting beliefs.

As explored in our previous chapter, holding onto the past often leads to worry, rumination, and cycles of anxiety that diminish both your energy and your effectiveness. It traps leaders in a defensive posture - trying to avoid repeating mistakes instead of moving forward with courage.

Similarly, spending too much time in the future can create a different kind of paralysis. While vision and strategic foresight are important, dwelling too long on *what ifs* feeds overwhelm, stress, and fear of failure. The mind races ahead to problems that may never occur, leaving leaders feeling unanchored, reactive, and drained. This state makes it hard to inspire, to connect, or to lead with compassion and clarity.

By anchoring yourself in the present moment, you keep the leadership flow alive. You move with awareness, touching the past for wisdom, checking the future for alignment, but always acting from the now. This rhythm of movement mirrors the infinity symbol on the cover of this book - a continuous loop, flowing through time, centered always in the now.

Staying grounded in the present enables you to make better decisions, respond to challenges with calm clarity, and cultivate environments where others feel safe, valued, and inspired to grow.

When you notice where your focus lies and intentionally choose your state, you can reframe your thoughts and language to create empowering stories, moving through life with greater flow and achieving better outcomes.

Focus - Frame - Flow!

How To Get Back On Track

When you notice that things are not on an even keel and are not sure why, ask yourself these questions to notice where you are at and identify one action you can take to get back on track.

- Where is my attention right now? (past, present, future)
- What am I focusing on?
- Am I getting *stuck* anywhere?
- What is the impact of this on me?
- What is the impact of this on my team?
- What's preventing me from flowing back to being present?
- What do I need to *stop* doing?

- What do I need to *start* doing?
- What is one action I can take NOW to be present?

One of the simplest ways to come back to being present is through engaging all of your senses in that moment.

The Authentic Leader's Reset: A 5-Sense Grounding Exercise

When leaders get caught between regrets about yesterday's decisions or anxiety about tomorrow's challenges, they lose their most powerful asset: Presence. This exercise uses your five senses as anchors to pull you back into the here and now, where authentic leadership actually happens.

This takes between 3-5 minutes and can be done anywhere - your office, a meeting room, even your car. Use before making important decisions, during stressful transitions, or whenever you notice your mind wandering to past failures or future worries.

Method

Step 1: SIGHT (5 things)

Identify **five specific things you can see** right now. Really observe them - the texture of wood grain on your desk, how light falls across your screen, or maybe the exact color of your coffee mug.

Great leaders are observers first. This step sharpens your ability to notice details others miss.

Step 2: TOUCH (4 things)

Notice **four different textures or sensations** you can feel - your chair against your back, the temperature of air on your skin, the weight of your feet on the floor, or the texture of your clothing.

Leaders who are grounded in their physical presence command respect and project stability.

Step 3: SOUND (3 things)

Listen for **three distinct sounds** - the hum of air conditioning, voices in the hallway, your own breathing, or the traffic outside.

Authentic leaders are skilled listeners. This step attunes you to the subtle communications happening around you.

Step 4: SMELL (2 things)

Take a deeper breath and identify **two scents** - coffee aroma, fresh air from a window, cleaning products, or even just the neutral smell of your environment.

Scent is closely linked to memory and emotion. This step helps you access your intuitive intelligence.

Step 5: TASTE (1 thing)

Focus on **one taste** in your mouth - the aftertaste of coffee, minty freshness from toothpaste, or simply the neutral taste of your saliva.

Taste requires you to turn attention inward, connecting you with your gut instincts, a leader's most valuable compass.

After engaging all five senses, take one final deep breath and ask yourself: **"Who am I being in this moment as an Authentic Leader?"** Allow the answer to emerge naturally.

You're now fully present and ready to lead from authenticity rather than anxiety or regret.

Making The Method A Leadership Habit

Use this technique before important meetings, after receiving difficult news, or when transitioning between major tasks. You can even schedule this exercise two to three times per week to practice it, so it becomes part of your toolkit. Consider leading your team through this exercise at the start of challenging group discussions. When everyone is being present, you get more group cohesion, better creativity, and greater innovation.

This exercise works by activating your parasympathetic nervous system, calming the fight-or-flight response that often accompanies leadership stress.

By deliberately engaging each sense, you're telling your brain: "I am safe, I am here, I am ready to respond."

Remember: Authentic leadership isn't about having all the answers - it's about being fully present to ask the right questions and discover the best responses.

7. Managing Your Time And Energy With Intention

Authentic Leaders understand that time and energy are not just resources to manage - they are reflections of your priorities, your mindset, and ultimately your leadership presence. Where you place your time and where you invest your energy sends a clear message: *This is what matters. This is where we lead from.*

Many leaders we work with initially hold the belief that time runs them. That there's never enough. That they are *time poor*. This belief system doesn't just shape your schedule; it shapes how you feel at the end of the day - drained, reactive, and stuck in cycles of exhaustion.

As we've explored in previous chapters on Mindset and Supercharging Your Language, the words you use matter. When your language revolves around lack - "I don't have enough time," or "I'm just so busy"- your brain will find evidence to reinforce that reality.

A simple but profound shift happens when leaders consciously change their language. Replacing *busy* with *productive, chaotic* with *purposeful,* and *I have to* with *I choose to,* can transform not only your mindset but how you approach your day and how you feel at the end of the day. You get to choose this transformation.

Pausing between tasks - even for 10 seconds - allows your nervous system to reset, your mind to refocus, and your energy to replenish. These micro-pauses of intention accumulate throughout the day, leaving you more energized, more present, and far less reactive by the time you close your laptop or the door.

This links beautifully with the infinity flow we introduced earlier. Anchoring yourself in the present allows you to consciously touch on the past (what worked, what drained you), glance toward the future (where you're heading), and then make powerful decisions in the now. It also allows for being more resourceful and innovative, creating different perspectives to enhance your well-being as a leader.

Ed Mylett has a different perspective on time management, proposing that each 24-hour day can actually contain three distinct days within it. Instead of viewing time as a single, linear stretch, he divides his day into three focused eight-hour segments; one dedicated to work and productivity, one to relationships and connection, and one to health, rest, and personal growth. By reframing time this way, Mylett creates multiple opportunities within a single day to reset intentions, celebrate wins, and course-correct.

This mindset disrupts the traditional narrative of being *too busy* or *running out of time*, and instead empowers leaders to design their days with intentionality and balance. It invites a shift from time scarcity to time abundance, where each segment becomes a fresh chance to lead consciously, make meaningful progress, and honor wellbeing.

For leaders striving to model sustainable high performance, Mylett's approach demonstrates that success is not about doing more in less time, but about creating more meaningful moments within the time we have. This is one example of how leaders are rethinking what's possible.[35]

This concept isn't about adopting a formula (unless you choose to), it's about expanding your sense of possibility. *Anything* is possible when it

---

[35] Mylett E. *The Power of One More: The Ultimate Guide to Happiness and Success.* Hoboken (NJ): Wiley; 2022.

comes to time and energy management, if you're willing to challenge old assumptions and lead yourself differently.

Ultimately, what matters is that you lead your time, energy, and attention with awareness. Whether that's through redefining your language, creating pauses to reset, or experimenting with new ways of structuring your day, these are conscious choices you get to make.

This is how you move from feeling at the mercy of time to *becoming the architect of your day.*

Mindset Shifts To Strengthen Your Time And Energy:

- From scarcity to abundance: "I always have enough time."
- From reaction to reset: "Each part of my day is a fresh start."
- From exhaustion to renewal: "Energy is a resource I protect and replenish."

When you lead yourself this way, you model a more sustainable, human, and empowered approach for others. One that keeps you connected to purpose, present in the moment, and energized for what truly matters.

8. The Art Of Pre-Framing And Re-Framing With Influence And Integrity

Authentic Leaders Understand This Truth:

The way you frame any conversation shapes the outcomes before a single word is spoken. Framing is not just a technique; it is a conscious leadership choice. It is the art of setting context with clarity, purpose, and integrity, inviting others into a space where influence, innovation, and solutions thrive.

Pre-Framing: Creating A Future People Want To Step Into

Pre-framing is about establishing the parameters, boundaries, and expectations upfront, intentionally shaping how others think, feel, and behave in the space you lead. Whether it's a conversation, a meeting, a relationship, or a decision, pre-framing sets the tone for success.

When done well, it invites people to engage fully and contribute meaningfully, but when it is done poorly, it primes people for resistance, frustration, or limitation.

Consider these two examples:

- "These next 45 minutes are going to be really tough. We've got a problem to solve, and this past decision is losing us money."

This pre-frame signals hardship, struggle, and risk. It shrinks possibilities before anyone has even begun to think creatively.

- The alternative is: "For the next 45 minutes, we get to focus on crafting solutions for this opportunity we've identified. Everyone's ideas are valuable. Together, let's find ways to 10x the value we offer this client."

This is an **Authentic Leadership pre-frame**. It invites possibility, innovation, ownership, and aligned contribution. Your words matter. The way you pre-frame creates the culture and energy in the room: open or closed, inspired or flat, forward-focused or stuck.

Pre-framing allows you to:

✓ Establish shared expectations.
✓ Shape the emotional and psychological climate.
✓ Anchor people in purpose and possibility.
✓ Lead with clarity, not control.

Pre-frames can be carried out before 1-1s, meetings, and even when presenting to a large audience. It sets the parameters with authenticity, openness, and transparency, not to constrict, but to enhance. Similar to boundaries, pre-framing is an incredible, vital skill for Authentic Leaders to master.

You're not constraining others; you're guiding them to success, aligned with purpose and values.

Re-Framing: Guiding People Back With Clarity And Care

Even with a strong pre-frame, conversations can veer off-track. Authentic Leaders use re-framing not as correction, but as a gentle realignment. Re-framing brings people back to the purpose with integrity and respect.

Here's an example:

"As we agreed at the beginning, we're here to work through options for dealing with this client. We want to explore options and clarify our next steps. Let's stay focused on exploring these specific options."

Re-framing reminds people of the *shared intention*. It anchors them to the agreed purpose. It prevents drift, without shutting people down.

Influence Through Conscious Language

When you master pre-framing and re-framing, you step fully into your leadership responsibility:

- You choose your thoughts first.
- You clarify your intention before you speak.
- You use *supercharged language* (see chapter 5) that inspires, influences, and uplifts.

This is not manipulation. It is authentic, transparent leadership that enhances outcomes for everyone involved.

Why This Matters In Authentic Leadership

Pre-framing and re-framing are skills that elevate your ability to lead with integrity, even in challenging moments. They allow you to hold boundaries with *respect and confidence*, rather than fear or people-pleasing.

You no longer hesitate with thoughts like: I can't redirect them, they're more senior than me.

Instead, you calmly lead with: *This is the framework we agreed upon, so let's return to it.*

Authentic Leadership requires clarity, courage, and conscious language. Pre-framing and re-framing provide the practical tools to embody these qualities in every interaction.

9. A Decision-Making Strategy That Works – Every Time

Authentic Leaders Don't Waste Energy In Limbo

Decision-making isn't hard when you have a clear strategy that cuts through the noise.

Yet so often we hear:

"I'm great at making small decisions, but the big ones? The ones that impact my career, my family, my future? They exhaust me. I flip-flop, I get advice from everyone (which only confuses me more), I make a pros and cons list, and still I stay stuck."

Sound familiar?

Indecision drains your energy, your confidence, and your influence. Authentic Leaders do not stay stuck in indecision. They have tools that help them make decisions fast, clean, and with integrity. This is one of those tools.

The 3-Step Decision-Making Strategy For Authentic Leaders

Whether it's a decision involving thousands of dollars or a simple calendar choice, this strategy works. Why? Because it cuts through emotion, procrastination, and other people's opinions, and anchors you back to your OWN clarity and power.

Step one: Set yourself up for success

Before you start, ensure you are in a space where you won't be disturbed. Be fed, hydrated, and fully present. This strategy is about tapping into your wisdom, not reacting from fear or lack.

Clarity only comes when you create the right conditions for it.

Step two: Write down your decision in ONE clear sentence

Examples:

- Am I going to have a courageous conversation with this underperforming team member?
- Am I going to pitch for this client project?
- Am I going to invest $12,000 into this coaching program?

Step three: Ask yourself these four questions (in this order):

1. What is the *worst* that can happen?
2. What is the *best* that can happen?
3. What is *most likely* to happen?
4. Can I live with *the worst?* (Yes *or* No).

The magic lies in question 4: If you can live with the worst, move forward. If you can't, adjust or redirect your focus.

Let's work this strategy through for the above real-world examples:

Decision	Best	Worst	Most Likely	Can I Live with the Worst?
Have a courageous conversation with an under-performing team member	We resolve the issue, work better together, and achieve our targets.	They get upset, disengage, or leave.	There will be emotions, and clarity emerges, where we find the next step forward.	YES: If they leave, they weren't the right fit. NO: We're too under-resourced right now to let anyone leave.
Pitch for a new client project	They love our proposal, become a long-term client, and refer others.	They reject the pitch.	They trial us with phase one.	YES: We learn, refine, and improve for the next pitch. NO: Our current priorities require full focus elsewhere.
Invest $12,000 in coaching	Life-changing growth, new results, expanded leadership toolkit.	Waste my time and money.	Valuable insights, growth, and some key tools gained.	YES: Growth is non-negotiable for my future success. NO: Financially not the right time — other priorities first.

That's it. Decision made. YOU GET TO CHOOSE.

This strategy is short, quick, and effective. It doesn't take weeks or months, unless you let it. You can make powerful decisions in minutes when you practice and trust this framework.

When you use this strategy, you eliminate:

- Emotional spirals
- Indecisiveness
- Limiting beliefs
- *What if...* overthinking

You get to decide quickly, powerfully, and then move on. That's Authentic Leadership.

10. How To Actively Celebrate Progress And Wins Along The Way

One of the greatest mistakes leaders make is waiting until the finish line to celebrate. They hold off recognition, praise, and celebration until the goal is reached, the project is completed, or the deal is signed. They tell themselves, "We'll celebrate when it's done."

Authentic Leadership doesn't operate on delayed gratification. High performance, sustained momentum, and human fulfilment thrive on celebrating progress in real-time, not just results at the end.

When you pause to acknowledge progress, when you notice the steps forward - no matter how small - you trigger a powerful neurochemical response in your brain. Dopamine is released. Energy lifts. Your motivation strengthens. Your brain says, *I want more of this.* This isn't simply about feeling good; it's about hardwiring yourself and your people for ongoing achievement, resilience, and engagement.

Celebration becomes the fuel for momentum, not the reward after exhaustion.

Authentic Leaders know this; waiting until the end to celebrate ignores the power of progress. It overlooks the daily wins, the moments of genius, the courageous efforts that deserve to be reinforced. It starves people of recognition in the very moments that help them build confidence, capability, and GRIT. Recognition in the moment sets people up to repeat their successes, to stretch further, to lean in when things get tough.

Celebrate The Steps, Not Just The Summit

Celebrating progress doesn't need to be elaborate. It can be as simple as a fist pump, a shared smile, a verbal acknowledgment, a social media post, a brief pause to say, "That was a breakthrough."

Or it can be grander; a team shout-out, a milestone celebration, a meaningful reward. What matters is not the scale of the celebration, but the **conscious choice to acknowledge the progress.**

Think of the leader writing a significant report or an academic paper, something that takes weeks, months, sometimes years. Waiting until the project is complete or the paper is published drains energy and motivation. It keeps people fixated on a distant outcome while ignoring the effort, the persistence, and the progress happening right now.

That's how burnout creeps in, how teams lose momentum, and how potential goes untapped.

Instead, break the journey into milestones and consciously acknowledge each one. Celebrate the completion of the structure, the clarity of the introduction, the finalization of the graphs, the alignment from the first collaboration meeting, or the approval of the budget.

Recognize progress not because it's perfect, but because it's forward movement. In doing so, you create a culture where progress is visible, valued, and inspiring.

Christine

I have always been someone who can celebrate *anything*, and I mean *anything*. I once high-fived myself in the mirror just for getting my to-do list started. Yep, not completed, just started! Because here's my truth: Celebration shifts your state. It ignites energy, and when your energy lifts, so does your ability to create next-level outcomes.

I remember one morning, I smashed out a few client notes, prepped for a workshop, and even managed to drink my coffee *while it was still hot*. That, my friends, was a win worth dancing for! So, I did. Right there in the kitchen. A full-on, solo, no-one-watching dance party. Why? Because when you condition yourself to celebrate the micro-wins, *you wire your brain to find progress everywhere.*

If we wait to celebrate only the big flashy milestones, or the next meeting, or next week, we miss out on the magic that's happening in between. And in those in-between moments, that is where our greatness is built.

Make sure you celebrate the *beejingas* out of everything: the early wake-up, the brave email, the tiny bit of clarity, the bold conversation. We get *one shot*, every single day, to create awesomeness.

Take it. Own it. Celebrate it.

When you actively celebrate along the way, you reinforce resilience (and bouncing forward). You elevate energy. You ignite the internal drivers that lead to greater productivity, deeper satisfaction, and heightened GRIT.

When you link celebration with GRIT, you create an unstoppable loop of progress and positivity. Every time you celebrate, you lock in the belief that effort matters. You signal to your brain, *Keep going - this works.* That's how you build unstoppable momentum.

Don't wait until the end. Celebrate now, because every small win is proof that your GRIT is alive, thriving, and leading you closer to greatness.

You remind yourself - and your people - that success isn't a destination. It's a series of moments well-lived, well-recognized, and well-celebrated.

Don't wait until the end. Celebrate now.

Bringing It All Together: Your Authentic Leadership Toolkit

This chapter provides you with some of the most valuable and impactful tools we teach leaders across the globe. Tools that transcend industries, roles, and organizational structures. These are the practical, proven strategies that help you lead with greater clarity, courage, and confidence, no matter the circumstances.

They work, but only if you *work them.* Authentic Leadership is not something you *know*; it's something you *DO* and *practice.* Mastery is built through consistent and conscious action. It is not capability which is about doing something well, mastery, as described by Sullivan and Hardy, is doing something *uniquely* well. Something that is uniquely yours, and yours alone![36]

These tools are designed to help you lead with intention, reduce stress, create momentum, and build environments where people, starting with yourself, can truly thrive.

They equip you to:

- Call Things *As Is* with Clarity and Compassion

---

[36] Sullivan D, Hardy B. 10x is easier than 2x: How world-class entrepreneurs achieve more by doing less. New York (NY): Hay House; 2023.

- Set and Hold Healthy *Boundaries*
- Have *Courageous Conversations*
- Run *Purposeful Meetings*
- Inspire Through *Clear Agendas*
- Stay Anchored in the *Present Moment*
- Manage Your *Time and Energy* with Intention
- *Frame Conversations* with Influence and Integrity
- *Make Decisions* with Confidence
- *Actively Celebrate* Progress Along the Way

At the heart of it all is this undeniable truth:

Leadership is a choice - moment by moment, thought by thought, word by word, action by action.

You *always* have a choice in how you show up, how you lead yourself, and how you influence others. Your mindset fuels your behaviors, your behaviors shape your impact and your impact defines your legacy.

Remember this: One *tiny tweak*, one small action each day, adds up to 365 powerful moments of progress in a year. That's how leadership mastery is built. Not through dramatic, one-off events, but through the consistent, deliberate practice of showing up just a little better, a little clearer, a little more courageously each day.

Approach this toolkit with curiosity, humility, and a growth mindset. Ask yourself regularly, *What can I do even better?* because when you lead yourself first - with authenticity, courage, and care - you become far better equipped to lead others to do the same.

Authentic Leadership is not just a skillset. It's who you are, what you do, and who you choose to become.

Your Toolkit Overview:

Core Focus Area	What It's About	Leadership Impact
Mindset Tools	Shape meaning, focus, and beliefs to lead with clarity and agency. *Meaning is created, focus directs energy, and beliefs fuel action.*	Leads with intentionality, resilience, and optimism.
Focus - Frame - Flow	Manage state, create empowering stories, and build effective strategies to achieve outcomes.	Brings calm, clarity, and structure to complex situations.
The Toxic Ten & Worthiness	Recognize and overcome internal patterns of fear, doubt, and unworthiness that block authentic action. *Procrastination, hesitation, impostor syndrome, stress, overwhelm, and more, all rooted in unworthiness.*	Reclaim your power by affirming your inherent worthiness. Essential inner work that unlocks your full leadership potential.
Focus	Focus on strengths, opportunities, and positive possibilities.	Builds a solutions-driven, high-energy culture.
Supercharge Your Language	Speak with ownership and purpose: 'I' language, positive self-talk, and empowering others through constructive dialogue.	Enhances trust, connection, and influence through words.
Self-Talk	Maintain empowering, future-focused internal dialogue.	Builds confidence, resilience, and persistence.
Communication with Others	Use inclusive, positive, and respectful language to foster collaboration.	Strengthens engagement, alignment, and psychological safety.
Leadership Action Tools	Practical tools to strengthen day-to-day leadership habits and behaviors.	Reduces overwhelm, increases consistency, and drives results.
Courageous Conversations	Speak openly and empathetically about difficult topics.	Builds trust, accountability, and clarity.

Core Focus Area	What It's About	Leadership Impact
Call It *As Is*	Communicate directly, clearly, and compassionately.	Creates transparency, trust, and swift progress.
Boundary Setting	Protect time, energy, and well-being through clear boundaries.	Maintains focus, reduces burnout, models self-respect.
Meetings & Agendas	Run purposeful meetings that drive action and alignment.	Increases efficiency, clarity, and engagement.
Time Management	Prioritize, plan, and protect time for what matters most.	Creates space for high-impact work and self-care.
Pre-Framing & Re-Framing	Shape conversations and expectations with influence and integrity.	Sets a positive tone, manages direction, and maintains momentum.
Celebrate Progress	Acknowledge wins along the way to fuel motivation and grit.	Builds momentum, engagement, and sustained performance.

Chapter Takeaways:

Tools Help Mastery - Use the tools effectively and you can be even more efficient.

3-Step RAP Method - *Recognize* what is happening, *accept* the situation, give yourself *permission* to feel the feels.

Boundary Setting - Boundaries are to enhance, not to punish.

Courageously Converse - Have conversations with candor, set yourself up with courage, clarity, and confidence using the PRISM formula.

Purposeful Agendas Create Purposeful Meetings – Every agenda item must clarify what's needed: decision, discussion, information, who's leading, and the time allotted.

Meetings Focus on the Present and Future – Meetings are not about the past. Focus discussions on what's been learned and what happens next.

Only Meet When It Matters – If there's no need for discussion or decision, there's no need for a meeting. Respect your team's time.

Shared Responsibility – Every person in the room is responsible for how they show up to the meeting. All must be prepared and ready for what is to come.

Anchor Yourself in the Present – Your greatest leadership influence exists in the now. Being present is where calm, clarity, and creativity live.

Flow Through Time – Use the past for learning, the future for direction, and the present for leadership and aligned action. This keeps you centred, clear, and effective. (The infinity symbol).

The 5-Sense Grounding Reset – Use sight, touch, sound, smell, and taste to bring yourself fully into the moment. Reset, when feeling stressed.

Manage Your Time and Energy with Intention – Time and energy are reflections of your priorities. What you focus on shows what you value, so choose consciously, purposefully and intentionally.

Shift from Scarcity to Abundance – Replace *I don't have time* with *I choose where I spend my time.* Language creates your reality.

Pre-Framing for Success – Effective pre-framing builds ownership and engagement from the start. Set standards upfront to create the parameters and shared purpose.

Re-Framing with Care – When discussions get off track, realign them back to purpose. Re-framing is leadership in action and it restores focus without diminishing others.

Decide with Clarity – Decision making can be easy, You get to choose.

The 3-Step Decision Making strategy – Set yourself up, clarify the decision to be made, ask yourself what is the best/worst/most likely outcome, then ask: "Can I live with the worst?" If yes — act. If no — adjust.

Celebrate Progress and Effort, Not Just Outcomes – Don't wait for the finish line. Recognize small wins consistently along the way, to fuel motivation, energy, and resilience.

Celebration Builds GRIT – Each moment of celebration releases dopamine, wiring your brain to do *the thing* again.

GRIT Grows Through Acknowledgement – Passion and perseverance thrive when effort is noticed. Every act of acknowledgment strengthens resilience and drives sustainability.

Leadership in Action – Authentic Leadership is who you *BE* and built on small, consistent actions.

Consistency Creates Legacy – Leadership isn't what you know, it's what you practice daily. One small action, done with integrity, adds up to extraordinary impact over time.

Section Three: HAVEing

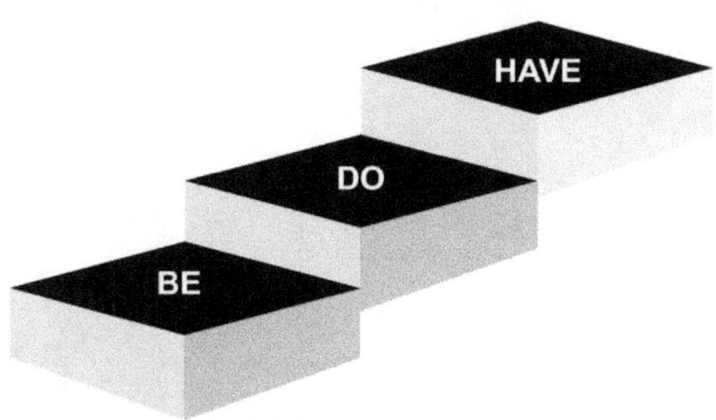

HAVEing *is more than a possession, it's a declaration. It's the point where vision takes form, where the abstract becomes tangible, and where the choices you've made about who you are BEing and what you are DOing crystallize into reality. In Authentic Leadership, HAVE is not about accumulation, it's about alignment.*

Too often, people drift through life without clarity about what they want to have. They settle for vague ambitions or borrowed definitions of success. They chase titles, money, or approval, hoping that one day those things will finally make them feel whole. But when you allow others to decide what you should pursue, you hand them the remote control of your life. You live reactively, not intentionally.

To HAVE as an Authentic Leader, is to claim ownership of your vision. It means asking boldly: What do I want my leadership to produce? What impact do I want to create? What do I want my health, wealth, and happiness to look like, on my terms?

The danger of ignoring this pillar is simple: without defining your HAVE, you remain busy and unfulfilled. Authentic Leaders dare to design their destination. They understand that true wealth is measured by opportunities created, health by energy sustained, and happiness by the quality of their daily experience.

The power of HAVEing lies in clarity. Define it, own it, and let it fuel every step of your leadership journey.

CHAPTER 7

To Have Health, Wealth, And Happiness

"The future belongs to those who believe in the beauty of their dreams."
—*Eleanor Roosevelt*

The Power Of HAVEing: Defining Success Through Authentic Leadership

Christine

I want to start with a truth that might rattle you a little: If you don't know what you want to *have*, you've essentially given other people the remote control to your life.

Think about it. If you can't articulate clearly what you want to have, what you want to experience, achieve, feel, or create, then you are letting others decide for you. You're sailing through life at the mercy of winds that aren't your own. You get pulled into their ideas, their expectations, their definitions of success. You say "yes" when you mean "no" just to stay approved of or just to fit in. You stop being your true self.

Authentic Leadership demands that you cut the wires on that remote control. *Snip!* Take control back. Take *ownership* of your life.

When "HAVE" Became Real For Me

Let me share a personal story.

Years ago, as an elite athlete, I was obsessed with what I thought I *needed* to have: the perfect training program, flawless competition results, or the approval of coaches and selectors. I thought if I could just *get* those things, I would finally feel like I had arrived.

But what actually happened was, the harder I chased those external markers, the emptier I felt. My body started breaking down. My mindset spiralled into self-doubt, and instead of easing up or taking a step back, I pushed and pushed.

It wasn't until I shifted from **need** to **want** that everything changed.

I started asking myself: "What do I want to gain from this sport? Who do I want to become through it? What do I want my life to look, sound and feel like beyond the team?"

That shift unlocked freedom. It gave me permission to value my health, to redefine wealth as opportunity rather than as medals, and to pursue happiness - not as a reward on the scoreboard, but as something I got to cultivate daily.

When I let go of chasing what I "needed," my performance actually improved.

That lesson has carried through every stage of my career and into the work we do at WALT Institute. HAVEing is never about what you collect externally, it's about who you become, who you BE internally, and what you consciously choose to integrate into your Success Zone.

The Have Component Of Be – Do – Have

You have already explored who you choose to BE as an Authentic Leader. You already know what you must DO, the actions, habits, and courageous conversations that flow from that identity.

Now we arrive at the third pillar: HAVE.

This is the part where everything comes together.

This third pillar, HAVE, is often misunderstood. Many leaders mistakenly equate *having* with external possessions: the job title, the salary, the recognition, the corner office. And while those things might come along the way, they are not the true markers of *HAVEing* for an Authentic Leader.

The Trap Of Living Backwards

When we talk about leadership, so much of the conversation gets stuck on what we *do*. Most people get this formula upside down. They live life in reverse. We're constantly bombarded with "How are we going to do this?", given advice about what actions to take, what strategies to follow, or what checklists to tick off to be considered a *successful leader*.

But the Be-Do-Have model reminds us that leadership is not just about what you are *DOing*, it's about who you *are BEing*, and ultimately, what you choose to *HAVE*.

Most people live life backwards. They chase the *have*:

- *When I have the promotion, then I'll BE confident.*
- *When I have a million dollars, then I'll BE secure.*
- *When I have more time, then I'll be able to prioritize my health and family.*

Do you see the trap?

They believe that by getting the *have*, they'll finally be able to *do* the things that bring fulfillment, and eventually *be* the person they dream of. But that's not how it works. The model flips. It starts with *BEing*, flows into *DOing*, and results in *HAVEing*.

To even begin the journey of having amazing leadership abilities, you must *define* what you *want* to have. Without clarity about the destination, the path makes no sense.

If you don't know what you want to *have*, you end up running in circles, working harder, and achieving less. You get tossed around by other people's agendas. You become a drifting leader, reactive, easily pulled off course, and constantly feel behind.

Imagine a ship on the ocean without a compass that doesn't know where it's headed. What a fruitless exercise that would be, and one that would end badly.

To *have* as an Authentic Leader is about clarity. It's about knowing, with conviction, what you want your life, your leadership, and your impact to look like. It's about being intentional rather than drifting. It's about *defining success on your terms*, not by someone else's playbook.

When you are clear about what you want to *have*, everything sharpens. Your focus intensifies. Your energy aligns. You move from survival response to vision, and you begin to live and lead from a place of purpose.

Living By Need vs. Living By Want

One of the clearest distinctions I've seen in my years of coaching and training is this: Some leaders live by *need*, while others live by *want*.

Leaders who live by *need* are constantly firefighting and reactive. Their questions sound like this:

- "What do I need to do to meet their expectations?"
- "How do I manage these people?"
- "How do I meet my KPIs?"

This is exhausting. It's small. It's reactive. It's suffocating. Living by *need* keeps you trapped in survival mode; and when you are in survival mode, you cannot access your highest levels of creativity, vision, or courage.

I've seen so many leaders burn out because they live by need. They resent their roles. They blame others. They start shrinking their future down to the size of their immediate problems. They lose their spark.

Living and leading from *need* is fear-based. It's rooted in scarcity, lack, and a belief that, "I just need to make do." When we believe we *should* be grateful for what we already have and *shouldn't* ask for more, we unconsciously lower our standards and cut ourselves off from possibility.

Authentic Leaders get to live by *want*. They expand their horizons. They ask bigger, more generative questions:

- "What do I *want* for this team?"
- "What do I *want* to create?"
- "What kind of impact do I *want* us to have?"

Want is expansive. It pulls you forward. It ignites creativity and magnetizes opportunities. It inspires others to commit and rise with you.

Dan Sullivan, the world's top entrepreneurial coach, puts it beautifully in his co-authored book with Benjamin Hardy, *10x Is Easier Than 2x*: "Need is small. Want is big. All progress starts by telling the truth: what do you really want?"[37]

The truth is, most leaders don't give themselves permission to want. They don't even ask the question. They feel guilty for wanting more.

They think, *Who am I to say I want this? Shouldn't I just be grateful for what I have?*

But gratitude and desire are not opposites. You can be deeply grateful for what you have *and* want more. In fact, that's what growth is all about.

So here's the question you get to ask yourself right now: "Do I want to be an Authentic Leader who creates meaningful impact?"

When you decide what you *want* with clarity, then you get to claim your power back and create it.

You Can't Hit What You Haven't Set

Clarity is power. If you don't know what you want to have, you'll never create it. You'll drift into other people's expectations, agendas, and measures of success.

---

[37] Sullivan D, Hardy B. *10x is easier than 2x: How world-class entrepreneurs achieve more by doing less.* New York: Hay House; 2023.

This is one of the most common traps I see with leaders. They spend years climbing the ladder, only to reach the top and realize the ladder was leaning against the wrong wall. They achieved someone else's version of success, not their own.

Authentic Leadership invites you to pause and ask:

- What do I actually *want* to have in my leadership?
- What do I *want* my days to look like?
- What kind of impact do I *want* to leave behind?
- What do I *want* this to feel like at the end of each day/year?

Notice that last one: *feel like.* Too often we only define success in terms of what it looks like on paper; the job title, the accolades, the numbers. But leadership is lived, felt, *and* experienced. If your leadership doesn't *feel* aligned, sustainable, and meaningful, then it doesn't matter how it looks.

You can't hit what you haven't set. If you don't define what you want to *have,* your leadership becomes a moving target, always out of reach, and you end up drifting, not directing.

Drifting vs. Directing

Drifting is easy. It's what happens when you let external noise, your boss's demands, the organization's agenda, or the latest urgent fire, dictate your every move. But drifting leaders don't build legacies; they simply maintain the status quo.

Directing leaders, *Authentic Leaders,* choose differently. They get clear on what they want to have, declare it, and set their own standards. They lead from intention, not reaction.

When you direct your vision, you stop lurching from crisis to crisis and start leading with clarity and purpose. This creates freedom for you, and your team. People trust leaders who know where they're going and invite others to rise with them.

Clarity is magnetic. It aligns who you are (*BEing*), what you do (*DOing*), and what you ultimately have (*HAVEing*). When that alignment clicks, everything shifts: your energy, your influence, and your impact.

The Big Three Wants: Health, Wealth, And Happiness

When you peel back the layers of human desire, most things fall into three broad categories: health, wealth, and happiness.

Now, I'm not talking about abstract concepts. I'm talking about *your* version of these things, defined by you, and lived by you. My definition of health, wealth, and happiness won't be the same as yours, and that is just perfect.

Let's break them down.

Health

Health is often reduced to eating clean, exercising, and sleeping well. But true health is multidimensional. It encompasses:

- *Physical health*: Energy, strength, mobility, stamina. The ability to move your body with freedom and confidence.
- *Mental health*: Focus, clarity, calm. The capacity to manage stress, think strategically, and stay resilient under pressure.
- *Emotional health*: Emotional intelligence, regulation, and the ability to connect with yourself and others authentically.
- *Spiritual health*: A sense of meaning and alignment, however you define it, connection to purpose, values, and something greater than yourself.

For some, having health might mean finishing a marathon. For others, it's being able to get through a 12-hour workday without collapsing. For another, it's the simple joy of playing with their kids on the floor without pain.

Your health is your foundation. Without it, nothing else is sustainable.

Wealth

Wealth is not just about money. It's about resources, options, and freedom. Money is finite (it runs out) but wealth is infinite, ever abundant and we create it from a state of resourcefulness.[38]

Of course, financial security matters, but wealth is an infinite resource and comes in the form of:

- Wealth of *relationships*: Deep, supportive, energizing connections.
- Wealth of *knowledge*: Skills, expertise, and wisdom that no one can take away.
- Wealth of *time*: Having the space and flexibility to do what matters for you.
- Wealth of *influence*: The ability to use your voice, your position, your platform for good.

To me, wealth is about access. It's about knowing that resources, opportunities, and connections are available to me, and using them at a 10x level. In *The 10x Is Easier Than 2x* philosophy, 10x doesn't mean working ten times harder; it means thinking ten times bigger. It's about stepping beyond incremental growth and daring to design a completely different playing field.

When you operate at a 10x level, you stop asking, "How can I do more?" and start asking, "What would be extraordinary?"

You let go of the 80% that no longer serves you and focus on the 20% that truly moves the needle. You make decisions that align with your highest vision, not your current limitations. You choose the freedom to want, and then create it!

---

[38] Sullivan D, Hardy B. 10x is easier than 2x: How world-class entrepreneurs achieve more by doing less. New York (NY): Hay House; 2023.

That's real wealth. The ability to choose your future, not react to it. When you have wealth, you have choices, and choice is the purest form of freedom.

Happiness

Happiness has layers. There's the short-term pleasure kind, like eating gelato on a hot summer day. Then there's the deeper satisfaction kind, like knowing you've made a difference in someone's life. Then there's what Aristotle called *eudaimonia*: a flourishing life grounded in meaning, growth, and contribution. Martin Seligman describes it as meaning beyond self, or *Altruism*.[39]

To have true happiness is to feel aligned. It's living in a way where your actions and values match. It's waking up each morning with a sense of energy and optimism, and going to bed at night with a sense of contentment.

And yes, happiness is personal. For one person, it's adventure and thrill. For another, it's stability and peace. Both are valid.

When you take time to sit and write down what you *want* in each of these three areas (*Health, Wealth and Happiness*), you will then know where you are going and what you will have. Then, you can practice *BEing* that person now, allowing yourself to align in every way, and find that the *DOing* comes consistently and easily.

Practical Reflection: Defining Your "Have"

So let's define what you HAVE, together. Grab a journal, a blank page, or open a fresh document and write your answers to these prompts. Don't censor yourself. Don't worry about how. Remember, *the how always catches up.*

---

[39] Seligman MEP. *Flourish: A visionary new understanding of happiness and well-being.* New York (NY): Free Press; 2011.

Just be radically honest with yourself:

1. **What do I want to have in my leadership?**
   (Not what you think you should have, not what someone else wants you to have, what *you* want.) Keep asking; and what else, and what else…?

2. **What do I want to have in my daily experience as a leader?**
   (Energy, creativity, connection, autonomy? Define the *feeling states* as much as the outcomes.)

3. **What do I want to have in my impact?**
   (What difference do you want to make, or legacy do you want to leave, in your organization, community, or world?)

4. **What do I want to have in my relationships as an Authentic Leader?**
   (Trust, collaboration, openness, respect - be *really* specific.)

Once you've written this down, read it back to yourself. Does it light you up? Does it expand you? If it feels too small, too safe, or too much like someone else's agenda, go deeper. Push further.

Allow yourself to *want*.

Authentic Leadership begins with clarity of vision. Decide what you *want* to *have*. Own it. Write it. Speak it. And then go and create it.

Breaking The "I Can Have This OR That" Conditioning

Here's where I get fired up.

Most of us have been trained since childhood to believe life is about *either/or*. You can have this or that. Not both.

- You can have the lollies (candy) OR the chips.

- You can have the TV OR the piano.
- You can have success OR freedom.
- You can have health OR wealth.

We carry this conditioning into adulthood, until it becomes a rigid pattern of belief and behaviors that we are not aware of. We believe that if we focus on our career, our health just has to suffer. If we build wealth, then our relationships will always fall apart. If we chase happiness, then we won't be taken seriously.

But what if that's a lie? What if you can have this *AND* that?

And what if it doesn't even stop there?

What if you can have this AND that AND that AND that?

What if you can have it all?

Not in the shallow hustle-culture way of *having it all* where you work yourself into the ground trying to juggle everything at once. But in the authentic way, where you align your *BEing*, your *DOing*, and your *HAVEing*, so that health, wealth, and happiness expand together.

The Belief Shift

To live this way, you have to make a fundamental mindset and belief shift. You have to stop seeing life as a series of trade-offs and start seeing it as a *series of choices* and *decisions* that you get to make.

It's not: *I can either have a strong body OR a successful career.*
It's: *I choose to be the kind of leader who has both.*

It's not: *I can either be financially free OR deeply connected in my relationships.*
It's: *I choose to be the kind of leader who creates both.*

This isn't about knowing it intellectually. Plenty of people will read this and nod along: *Yeah, yeah, I know that.* But knowing is not enough! You have to *embody* it. You have to *believe* it, at a cellular level, that you *are allowed to have it all.*

The truth is that you have already beat the odds. You are already on this planet. This means that you had over a *one in four trillion* chance of being alive. Wow, take a moment to think this through. You were meant to be here. You are incredibly amazing. You were *BORN worthy*!

Why waste your time living someone else's life?

The Success Zone

Having what you want is rarely about staying comfortable. If you *be* the same person and *do* the same things, you will *have* the same results.

To have *different* results, *you must step into your Success Zone.*

This isn't about leaping into panic or chaos. It's not about grinding yourself into exhaustion. The Success Zone is the space where growth happens. It's the stretch zone, the space just beyond comfort, where you start to think, act, and see things differently.

In this zone, opportunities appear that you couldn't see before. Conversations shift. Possibilities expand. Opportunities arise. You start creating the conditions for health, wealth, and happiness to flow.

The Authentic Leader's Declaration

One of the ways to cement what you want to have is to write it down, practice it, see it often, and declare it as truth.

I want you to do this exercise right now! Write your own "I have" declaration. It might sound like this:

- *I have* a high-performing team with me that thrives in trust and connection.
- *I have* a flexible, strong body that gives me energy every day.

- *I have* absolute financial freedom, where money flows easily and is a tool for impact.
- *I have* recognition for my genius and the ability to change lives.
- *I have* laughter, joy, and adventure every day with the people I love.

Notice how expansive this feels. There are no trade-offs here, just possibilities.

You Can Have It All

To be an Authentic Leader is to *stop* living by someone else's script. It is to *stop* giving away the remote control to your life, and to *start* living in alignment with who you truly *BE* and what you want.

When you decide what you want to *have,* and you align your *being* and *doing* with clarity, you unlock flow. You live in abundance. You experience more ease, more joy, more freedom.

Living every day, experiencing Health, Wealth, and Happiness, begins with a set of choices. A choice of what you focus on, a choice of who you be, and a choice of what you do. You don't have to settle, play small, or consider trading-off to get the things you want.

By following the principles in this playbook, you get to create the life you choose, AND you can have it all!

Chapter Takeaways:

Having as Alignment – *HAVEing* is not about possessions; it's the visible alignment between who you are *BEing* and what you are *DOing*.

Clarity Creates Power – If you don't know what you want to *HAVE*, you will never create it.

Define Success for Yourself – As an Authentic Leader, you get to define what success means to you. Create their own measures of health, wealth, and happiness.

Dimensions of *HAVEing* – True success integrates physical, mental, emotional, and spiritual wellbeing.

From Need to Want – Living by *need* keeps you reactive; living by *want* expands creativity, choice, and freedom.

Be → Do → Have – The authentic success formula flows from *BEing*, to *DOing*, to *HAVEing*, not the other way around.

Write Your 'I Have' Statements – Declaring what you want to *HAVE*. Only then can you create the anchors for intention, direction, and alignment.

No Trade-Off Thinking – You can have health and wealth and happiness simultaneously.

Find Your Success Zone – Growth happens in the stretch between comfort and challenge. This is your zone of expansion.

CHAPTER 8

Sustaining Yourself And Your Authentic Leadership

"Rest and self-care are so important. When you take time to replenish your spirit, it allows you to serve others from the overflow. You cannot serve from an empty vessel." —Eleanor Brownn

Sustaining yourself and looking after your health and energy is such an obvious thing to do, yet, so many leaders fail to do it.

If you want to have the career and life you want, then sustainability, ongoing development and practicing what you *preach* is a *must*.

Every day that we coach, we connect with people who say "Yes, but."

- "Yes, I know I should prioritize sleep, but there is just so much to do."
- "Yes, I am pro work/life balance, but I just can't seem to do it for myself."

Why Is That?

Let's agree right here, right now, that it's prudent to look after ourselves first. Like the frequently used analogy, you need to put on your own oxygen mask *first*, before you help others. Quite frankly, if you are unable to breathe, then you cannot help anyone else.

This is the starting point. We *know* this, but do we *believe* this, and do we *follow through*? If we truly believed this to be true, then no problem. We would all be doing it, consistently, effectively and be reaping the rewards with ease.

Let's explore the BS beliefs that hold us back (remember BS stands for Belief Systems, Blind Spots, and Bullsh*t).

Here is a three-step formula to explore where you are at.

The Full Tank Formula To Fill Up Your Cup

Leadership isn't a sprint, it's a marathon powered by how well you care for yourself *every single day*. Just like an athlete can't perform without refueling, a leader can't show up fully without a *full tank* of self-care, self-nurturing, and sustainable energy.

This formula is designed to help you recognize where you're running low, call out the stories that keep you drained, and build practical habits that keep your tank topped up, so you can lead with clarity, resilience, and authenticity. To HAVE a full tank, you must DO things that will fill up your tank and to do those things you must BE the person who aligns, believes, and embraces the Full Tank Formula.

We all know: *You cannot pour from an empty cup.*

Let's get into the three steps of *The Full Tank Formula*; your roadmap to sustained Authentic Leadership and wholehearted living.

The Full Tank Formula

Step One: Recognize and Reveal

Before you can change how you lead, you first need to shine a light on the patterns and beliefs running the show. Awareness is the foundation; without it, you're just reacting on autopilot.

- Ask yourself:
  1. *What story am I telling myself about why I 'can't' prioritize my own needs?*
  2. *What would happen if I challenged that story as a complete lie?*
  3. *Who would I BE without that story?*

- Be radically honest, no sugar-coating.
- Notice how often your story starts with; I *can't because...* or *I have to but...* These are clues to the BS (Belief Systems, Blind Spots, Bullsh*t).
- Write your answers down so you can see them in black and white. Clarity lives on paper, not just in your head.

Step Two: Interrupt and Reframe

Now that you've called out your BS, it's time to challenge it in real time and replace it with something that actually serves you.

- Ask: "What is the opposite of that BS belief?"
- Craft a *new empowering statement* that supports your well-being and leadership.
- Choose *one micro-shift* you can implement this week to prove the new belief true (e.g., *I protect my sleep so I can show up at my best,* paired with a non-negotiable bedtime).
- The aim here is to *rewrite the mental code* so your default reaction changes over time.

Step Three: Act and Anchor

Knowledge without action is just self-help. This is where you embody the new belief until it becomes second nature.

- Commit to and act on one daily self-care habit that reinforces your new belief.
- Share your commitment with an accountability partner or coach so you can't hide when it gets uncomfortable.
- Anchor it: Celebrate every time you honor your new self-care standard, small wins compound into big results.
- Reflect weekly: "How did I lead differently because I looked after myself first?"

Remember: When you define what you did differently, celebrate it. Put a smile on your dial from ear to ear, stimulate those endorphins, stack your goodies, and remember how amazing you are!

Sustaining yourself is not optional, it's the bedrock of Authentic Leadership and lasting impact. When you intentionally nurture your mind, body, and spirit, you create a powerful ripple effect that elevates not only your own performance but also the well-being and engagement of everyone around you.

Too often, leaders think self-care is a luxury or something to squeeze in if there's time. But true leadership calls for a radical shift: Seeing self-care as a non-negotiable, strategic act of stewardship over your energy, resilience, and clarity.

This chapter invites you to lean into that shift through *The Full Tank Formula*; a practical, no-nonsense guide to breaking free from the limiting beliefs and hidden stories that drain you, and stepping fully into a sustainable way of leading that honors who you are, what you value, and the legacy you want to leave.

The only way to serve others powerfully and authentically is to lead from a place of fullness; a *full tank* of self-care, self-nurturing, and sustainable energy. As I have already shared, you do NOT want to be one of *those* leaders who burn out because they ignored the possibilities of what they could do differently, and did not consider the cost of *not stopping* the relentless push, drive and overload.

Six Types Of Leaders You DON'T Want To Be!

Leadership is as much about what you *don't* do as what you *do*. It's easy to get caught in habits or mindset traps that drain your energy, undermine your effectiveness, or send confusing signals to your team.

In fact, some leadership style choices can quietly erode trust, stifle growth, and burn out both the leader and their people. These are the kinds of leaders whose behaviors you *don't* want to mirror, because they create more problems than solutions.

Below are six common leader personas that serve as cautionary tales. They are all fueled by one or more of the Toxic Ten, so when you rid yourself of those patterns, you are able to break through these personas.

Each offers a mirror for reflection. What habits or stories are creeping into your leadership that are holding you back from becoming the authentic, sustainable leader you aspire to be?

1. The Perpetual People-Pleaser – The Open-Door That Never Closes

This leader prides themselves on being *always available.* An open-door policy that means their door is never really *closed.* They are constantly interrupted, never get to their own work, get frustrated, and are exhausted at the end of each day but feel obligated to say *yes* to everyone. Their team respects them for being approachable, but over time, the leader's lack of boundaries breeds inefficiency, burnout, confusion, and blurred priorities.

2. The Holiday Hermit – The Leader Who Never Really Disconnects

They take vacations but stay *on call* 24/7, checking emails and troubleshooting issues from the beach or cabin. They believe stepping away fully will cause chaos, so they never truly refresh. Their team respects their dedication but learns to do the same, perpetuating a culture of constant availability, overwhelm, and low recharge.

3. The Ghost in the Office – Always Too Busy, Never Present

Physically present but mentally checked out, this leader is often *too busy* for meaningful conversations, coaching, or team connection. They hide behind their calendar, avoid courageous conversations, and never prioritize their own, or their team's well-being. They're reactive, disconnected, always *so busy*, and leave others wondering if they even care.

4. The Perfectionist Procrastinator - Waiting For The 'Perfect' Moment To Lead

They get stuck in over-planning, fear making mistakes, or wait for ideal conditions. As a result, decisions drag, opportunities slip away, and their teams feel stalled. They may neglect self-care because *there's always one more thing to fix.* The reality? Perfectionism fuels procrastination, blocks authentic action, and stifles true growth.

5. The Lone Wolf - I've Got to Do It All Myself

They pride themselves on outworking everyone else, staying late, working weekends, and carrying the load alone to prove their worth. Refusing to delegate or seek support, they wear exhaustion like a badge of honor. But the cost is steep: burnout, strained relationships, and a team starved of growth and connection. Their message is clear, sacrifice is success, yet it's an unsustainable facade that eventually cracks.

6. The Crisis Manager - Always in Fire-Fighting Mode

They thrive in chaos and urgency but neglect proactive self-care and planning. Constantly reacting to emergencies (rather than preventing them) drains their energy and clouds their vision. Their team feels the stress ripple down, and sustainable leadership falls by the wayside.

Why We Don't Want To Be These Leaders

Each persona reflects common traps that undermine not just the leader's well-being but the health and performance of their teams. They are just patterns we have created born from one or more of the Toxic Ten, and will cost us EVERYTHING. These leaders miss the mark on Authentic Leadership, which requires being present, establishing boundaries that enhance, engaging in activities of self-care, and setting intentions that influence.

Growth And Development: Continuous Learning And Conscious Expansion

When we talk about creating sustainable leadership, we are talking about far more than self-care and energy management. Sustainability also comes from the commitment to continuous growth and development, the conscious choice to keep evolving as a leader, human, and contributor to the world.

Without growth, leaders stagnate. Without conscious development, they fall into outdated patterns, relying on what *has worked* in the past rather than shaping what *will work* in the future.

True growth is not about passively attending a course once a year, taking notes, and leaving the resources to collect dust on a digital device. It is about daily learning opportunities, micro-adjustments, and intentional expansion.

As Authentic Leaders, we must ask ourselves: *What am I learning today? What am I implementing today? What micro-shift can I make that compounds over time into something extraordinary?*

The Neuroscience Of Authentic Growth

Neuro-encoding science shows us that every thought, belief, and behavior is etched into our nervous system. Neural pathways strengthen through repetition, whether they're pathways of avoidance, procrastination, or outdated leadership habits, or those of courage, accountability, and growth. What we practice becomes our default.

This means that every time you choose to step into feedback, apply new strategies, or experiment with a different approach, you are literally rewiring your brain toward sustainable, Authentic Leadership. Every time you default to fear, delay, or self-protection, you harden those circuits instead.

Growth, therefore, is not about accumulating more knowledge. Knowledge without application is simply intellectual entertainment. True growth happens only when knowledge is embodied, tested, and integrated into daily practice.

In Neuro-Linguistic Programming (NLP) terms, this is the shift from *conscious competence,* where you're deliberately practicing new skills, to *unconscious competence,* where those behaviors become part of who you are as a leader.[40]

The Neuroscience Of Modeling

Neuroscience also explains why *practicing what you preach* carries such weight. Human beings are wired with mirror neurons, the brain's system for observing and replicating others' behaviors. Your team learns as much by *watching you* as they do from what you say.

When you model authenticity, courage, and values-based action, your team unconsciously mirrors those behaviors. When you model avoidance, inauthenticity, or disconnection, those patterns ripple outward as well.

This is why Authentic Leadership is contagious. Your influence is not optional. The question isn't *whether* you are influencing people, but *how.*

Leaders who consistently embody authenticity anchor positive associations for their teams. Behaviors like speaking up, taking ownership, or practicing self-care become linked not with risk or fear, but with empowerment and growth. Over time, this rewires not just individual nervous systems, but the *collective culture.*

---

[40] Bandler R, Grinder J. *The structure of magic: A book about language and therapy.* Palo Alto (CA): Science and Behavior Books; 1975.

Authentic Leadership, then, is not about perfection, it's about presence. It's about courageously choosing growth over comfort, action over avoidance, and integrity over self-protection, knowing that every decision you make and every behavior you model leaves an imprint on the people around you.

Learning As A Daily Practice

Continuous learning does not need to be overwhelming. It is not about cramming more into an already overloaded calendar. Rather, it is about a mindset of curiosity and presence. Every interaction, every challenge, and every feedback loop becomes an opportunity to learn.

For example, instead of viewing courageous conversations as something to *get through,* an Authentic Leader reframes them as opportunities to learn about human behavior, emotional triggers, and communication effectiveness. When done with repetition and celebrated at the end of this process, this reframing experience rewires the brain to link challenge with growth rather than stress, making the process sustainable and energizing.

You *associate* courageous conversations with a positive experience that is about learning and growth, and therefore, set yourself up to keep doing this, more effectively, and with more ease.

These moments are short bursts of *micro-learning*: Quick, focused opportunities to learn and grow that can happen anytime, anywhere. They can be woven into conversations, actions, activities, or events. By making learning bite-sized and practical, micro-learning sets us up for continuous growth towards our goals through simple, achievable tweaks.

Examples of using micro-learning moments can be:

- Asking a trusted colleague: *"What's one thing I could do differently next time to be more effective?"*
- Reflecting for five minutes at the end of the day and asking yourself: *"What did I learn about myself today?"*

- Reading a short article or listening to a podcast, then immediately implementing *one practical idea* instead of just continuing to consume more content.

Sustainable leaders treat learning as a living practice speckled throughout the day, not as an occasional event.

The Power Of Feedback And Coaching

One of the fastest ways to accelerate growth is through feedback and high-level coaching. Left to our own devices, we are often blind to our own patterns. The brain filters information through existing beliefs and biases, which means we only see what confirms what we already think.

High-level coaches and trusted feedback partners help interrupt this loop.

A skilled coach does not simply give advice, they ignite thinking. They ask really impactful questions, and create a space for leaders to reflect, challenge assumptions, break out of habitual patterns and access new ways of thinking. Neuroscience research shows skilled coaching activates the Positive Emotional Attractor (PEA), engages the brain's *pre-frontal cortex*. This is the hub of creativity, resourcefulness, problem-solving, self-regulation and higher-order thinking. When this region is activated, leaders are far more able to generate innovative solutions, stay open and engaged, and move beyond the old, reflexive responses that keep them stuck.[41]

Here's the difference feedback and high-level coaching can make:

- A leader who never seeks feedback may unknowingly demotivate their team with rushed communication.
- A leader who regularly asks for feedback and works with a high-level coach learns to become more self-aware, more regulated and

---

[41] Boyatzis RE, Jack AI. The neuroscience of coaching. Consulting Psychol J Pract Res. 2018;70(1):11–27.

to slow down, listen actively, and communicate with clarity. This not only strengthens trust, but it also improves team performance.

The growth edge is never found in comfort zones. It is found in the uncomfortable and the uncertain - the Success Zone. Areas where others hold a mirror up to our blind spots.

Growth As Identity, Not An Event

One of the most powerful shifts Authentic Leaders can make is to move from seeing growth as an *event* - "I attended a leadership program" - to seeing growth as an *identity* - "I am someone who continuously grows and expands."

Identity drives behavior, and starts with who you say you are. In neuro-encoding terms, when you see yourself as a leader who learns and evolves daily, your unconscious mind seeks opportunities to align with that *identity*. It becomes easier to take action because your behavior is no longer something you force, it flows from who you believe yourself to be.

This is why embodying your "I am" statements or mindset resets, when used correctly, are so effective. They are not about empty positive thinking. They are about encoding a new identity into your neurology so that your actions follow naturally.

Practical Application For Authentic Leaders

To embed growth and development into sustainable leadership, consider these practices:

1. **Micro-Learning Daily:** Treat every challenge, feedback moment, or interaction as a chance to learn. Ask, "What did I learn from this?"
2. **Feedback Loops:** Regularly seek feedback from trusted colleagues or mentors. Don't wait for a specific time or process to be engaged, make it an ongoing practice.

3. **Work with a High-Level Coach:** A coach accelerates growth by expanding awareness, challenging limiting patterns, and helping rewire behaviors at the identity level.

4. **Implement Before Consuming More:** For every new insight you gain, apply it *immediately*. Successful leaders take immediate action. Don't move on to the next thing until you have implemented it.

5. **Identity Upgrade:** Reframe yourself: *I am a leader who grows daily.* Align your actions with this identity to strengthen sustainable behaviors.

From Knowledge To Embodied Growth

Ultimately, the commitment to growth and development is the commitment to sustainability itself. A leader who nurtures their energy through self-care but does not grow will *eventually plateau*. A leader who grows intellectually but never applies will accumulate information *without transformation*. Sustainable leadership requires both: The energy to show up fully and the willingness to grow continuously.

Information + focused, purposeful action = Transformation.

Remember, growth is not about perfection or arrival, it is about conscious expansion. It is about choosing curiosity over apathy, certainty over uncertainty, presence over autopilot, and implementation over accumulation.

When you make growth part of your daily rhythm, you not only sustain your own leadership, you also inspire those around you to grow, creating a ripple effect of Authentic, Empowered Leadership.

Practicing What You Preach

Something we are absolutely uncompromising about is *practicing what we preach*. Every principle, every tool, every strategy we've shared in this book: We live it, breathe it, and embody it daily.

We don't just talk about self-care, growth, and Authentic Leadership, we *do the work*. Because we know that if we are not walking this path ourselves, we have no right to guide you or the thousands of leaders we serve across the globe.

Do what I say has never created trust, influence, or transformation. But *watch what I do* and *see who I am being* is where real impact comes from. Authentic Leadership is not a performance; it's a lived experience.

The power of your leadership lies in the congruence between your words and your actions, your values and your choices. When who you *say you are* matches who you *actually are*, that is when you create influence, inspiration, and the kind of lasting impact that changes lives.

Application Of Learning

Learning without application is like a seed left in a packet. It has potential, but it never takes root or grows into what it was intended for. In the same way, leadership growth that isn't embodied in daily action becomes theoretical; a nice set of ideas that never truly impact lives. Sustainable Authentic Leadership requires not just learning, but living what you learn.

Putting knowledge into action is the essence of Authentic Leadership. It is the bridge between intention and impact. Anyone can speak about values, resilience, and purpose; fewer can consistently demonstrate them under pressure. The leaders who inspire deep trust and commitment are those whose *words and actions align*, even when it is difficult, inconvenient, or unseen.

This alignment creates powerful internal congruence. When what you think, feel, say, and do are in harmony, your nervous system operates in flow rather than conflict. People can sense this congruence. They may not be able to explain it in scientific terms, but they may intuitively feel whether a leader is embodying their values or simply talking about them. Incongruence erodes trust instantly, whereas congruence generates trust.

Walking The Talk

Authentic Leadership is not about perfection (see the Toxic Ten), it is about integrity.

When a leader *walks the talk*, they send an unspoken message to their team: *I don't expect anything of you that I am not willing to live myself.* This creates psychological safety, because people feel they are being led by someone real, not by a façade.

Consider a leader who tells their team to prioritize wellbeing but sends emails at midnight or 2 a.m. and never takes a holiday. The unspoken message is louder than the spoken one: *Do as I say, not as I do.* When you say one thing and do another, it results in a culture of burnout, masked by rhetoric about balance.

Now, imagine the opposite: a leader who models boundaries, schedules downtime, and encourages their team to do the same. A leader who refuses to be reactive when others' lack of priorities or incompetence creates an urgency that they *expect* the leader will fulfil.

This Authentic Leader normalizes self-care as a strength, not a weakness. They demonstrate the importance of being self-full and able to give to others from this fullness. The spoken and unspoken messages are aligned, and trust flourishes.

Application As Daily Integrity

Applying learning does not require dramatic gestures. It requires small, consistent choices that align with your values. Here are some ways leaders can embody what they preach:

- **If you value transparency:** Share the reasoning behind decisions, even when it's uncomfortable or unknown.
- **If you value growth:** Admit when you don't know something and show your willingness to learn.

- **If you value wellbeing:** Set boundaries around your own energy and support others in doing the same.
- **If you value collaboration:** Involve others in *problem-solving* instead of defaulting to 'telling them information' or control.

Each action becomes a micro-demonstration of integrity. Over time, these small signals compound into a culture of trust.

What we know to be true is that any outcome is not just one choice, it is a set of choices that create the outcome.

The Courage To Align

Practicing what you preach takes courage, because it often requires swimming against the current and even the crowd. Many organizations have unspoken norms that reward overwork, silence, and conformity. To model authenticity in such environments is to consistently challenge the status quo.

A leader who chooses to pause for reflection in a culture of busyness sends a signal that depth matters more than speed. A leader who openly shares their mistakes in a culture of perfectionism signals that vulnerability is strength and openness to learn. These choices are not always easy, but they are *always* powerful.

Congruence builds resilience. When your internal compass matches your external actions, you no longer waste energy on managing appearances. This frees up capacity for creativity, presence, and connection, qualities every sustainable leader needs.

A Story Of Embodiment

One leader we worked with recently, let's call her Sarah, recognized that while she spoke passionately about empowering her team, her behaviors often sent the opposite message.

She was quick to jump in and fix problems for her team rather than letting them experiment and learn. She often directed the pathway for every project, without allowing flexibility from the team's input. Through our high-level coaching, she began to see this pattern clearly.

Instead of just telling her team, "I trust you," Sarah began applying her learning in real time. She created space for her team to present solutions in team meetings, before offering her input. She resisted the urge to rescue, even when mistakes were made, and instead, used those moments as growth opportunities.

The transformation was remarkable. Within three months, her team began stepping up with confidence, ownership, and innovative ideas. Within six months, many in her team were shining bright, displaying strengths she never realized they had, and producing higher level outputs than before.

Sarah's shift was not just in words but in embodiment, and her team mirrored it.

Practical Application For Leaders

To apply your learning and practice what you preach, consider these steps:

- **Identify Core Values:** Write down your top five leadership values. Those things that are non-negotiables for you.
- **Audit Your Alignment:** Ask yourself, "Where am I living these values daily? Where am I out of alignment?"
- **Choose One Daily Action:** Pick one small behavior that demonstrates each value, and put these into action.
- **Seek Accountability:** Ask a high-level coach, mentor, or team member to give you feedback on how consistently you model your values.

- **Celebrate Embodiment:** Recognize and celebrate when you or your team align actions with stated values. This reinforces the behavior neurologically and culturally.

From Words To Impact

At its heart, practicing what you preach is about authenticity. It is about closing the gap between what you aspire to do, and what you embody. The leaders who leave legacies are rarely the ones with the most eloquent speeches. They are the ones whose *daily actions spoke louder than their words.*

Sustainable Authentic Leadership requires this kind of integrity. When you apply your learning, align your actions with values, and model authenticity, you create trust. Trust fuels connection. Connection fuels performance, and performance, when rooted in authenticity, is sustainable; not just for you but for everyone you influence.

Remember, Authentic Leadership is not about DOing a set of techniques, it is a lived expression of who you are BEing. If you want others to live authentically, begin with yourself. Model it. Embody it. Preach less, practice more.

Living What You've Learned

Sustaining yourself and your Authentic Leadership is not a nice-to-have, it is a non-negotiable. Rest, self-care, continuous learning, and daily embodiment of your values are the anchors that keep you steady in the relentless pace of leadership.

Without these foundations, you may achieve results in the short term, but at the cost of your health, relationships, and credibility.

Authentic Leadership calls you to play the long game, to build rhythms of renewal, growth, and congruence that ensure you not only survive leadership but thrive within it.

Know this: People do not follow what you say, they follow who you are.

Your team, your peers, and even your family watch the alignment between your words and actions more closely than you realize. This is why growth and application cannot remain theoretical. They must become visible, embodied, and consistent.

When you prioritize your energy, expand your capacity through learning, and practice what you preach, you give others permission to do the same. You create a ripple effect of resilience, empowerment, and authenticity that sustains not only you but also everyone you influence.

As we close this chapter, the invitation is simple: Choose one shift today! Maybe it is putting a boundary around your energy, maybe it is seeking feedback, maybe it is finally living out the value you've been talking about for years.

Whatever it is, act on it now. *DO* it today!

Authentic Leadership is sustained not by what you know, but by what you consistently live. The only way to serve powerfully, leave a legacy, and lead authentically is to lead from a place of fullness; so fill your tank, commit to your growth, and embody your truth.

Chapter Takeaways:

Lead from a Full Tank – You can't lead when running on empty. Authentic Leadership starts with a full tank mentally, emotionally, and physically. Self-care is being *self-full.*

Call Out the BS – Your Belief Systems, Blind Spots, and Bullsh*t stories drain you faster than any workload. Recognize them, rewrite them, and reclaim your energy.

Boundaries as Oxygen – Boundaries are there to enhance, not punish. Protect your time, energy, and focus. Because you deserve it!

Interrupt the Autopilot – Awareness creates choice, and choice changes everything. Notice the patterns, excuses, and habits that keep you in *busy mode*; choose a better path.

Growth as Identity – Growth isn't an event, it's who you are. Define your identity as; *"I am someone who continuously grows and expands.*

Model What You Teach – Your team learns more from what you *DO,* and who you *BE,* than what you say. Be the living example of boundaries, self-care, and integrity, that you want others to embody.

From Learning to Living – Knowledge that isn't applied is entertainment. Transformation only occurs when learning turns into consistent action.

Congruence Builds Credibility – When your words, values, and actions align, people trust you. Authentic Leadership is built in the gap between your talk and your walk.

Rest as a Power Play – Authentic Leadership calls you to play the long game. This means prioritizing rest, reflection, and renewal as the fuel that sustains your impact.

Leading Forward:

What's your one key takeaway from the chapter (of course there will be more), that you are going to take action on NOW?

CHAPTER 9

BE – DO – HAVE Authentic Leadership

"The players on your team are responsible for the vast majority of your leverage and ultimate success. Lousy players, poor leverage... business success is highly dependent on who you hire and who you don't fire."
—Keith J. Cunningham

The Sequence Of Authenticity

To HAVE authentic impact, you must first BE authentic, then DO in alignment with that BEing. This is the simple and powerful **BE → DO → HAVE** model.

The trap for so many leaders is trying to shortcut the process. They chase the HAVE, the results, titles, recognition, or external approval, without first embedding the BE. Without authenticity at your core, every result is fragile, every achievement hollow, and every interaction is likely to drain you.

As you step further and further into being an Authentic Leader, you get to constantly strengthen new habits and embed congruence into every area of your life. First, you BE authentic. Then, you DO the actions that reflect that authenticity. Only then do you HAVE the career, relationships, health, wealth, and influence that are sustainable.

When you live in full congruence with BE → DO → HAVE, you become *unstoppable*. Not from ego or arrogance, but from the deep certainty that clarity, confidence, and congruence bring.

Instead of asking, "What result can I get?", shift your thinking to:

- *What kind of person do I get to BE in this situation?*
- *Who do I choose to show up as, in this moment?*

These questions unlock authenticity, and from there, your actions align and the results take care of themselves.

BE – The Core Of Who You Are

Authenticity begins not with what you do, but with who you are BEing. It's not a tactic, it's an *identity*.

To BE authentic means anchoring yourself in values, integrity, and emotional congruence. It means stripping away masks and showing up as the same person in every room, with every person, in every moment. You BE your true genuine self. You get to dial up and dial down with congruence to create the best opportunity for you and *them* (anyone else you are working with or inspiring in that moment).

When you are grounded in who you are, Authentic Leadership flows naturally. Confidence is no longer a performance, it's your presence. Trust is no longer demanded, it's earned by simply being real.

Authentic Leadership starts with BEing yourself before doing anything else.

DO – Practicing Authenticity In Action, Consistently

Once you anchor into authenticity at your core, the next step is to embody it in everything you do. Every conversation, decision, and behavior becomes an opportunity to model authenticity.

This is where you *practice what you preach*. Authentic Leaders don't just talk about values, they live them. They don't just demand integrity from others, they demonstrate it in themselves. They have higher levels of effective communication, make better and faster decisions, and become a powerful and authentic *REAL* model.

Not just a role model, but a *REAL* model: A Resilient Empowered Authentic Leader.

When your actions align with who you are, trust multiplies. People no longer question your motives because they can see the congruence between your words and your actions. In leadership, every action is a message. The more aligned those messages are with your authentic self, the stronger your influence becomes.

Take Dean, who we have worked with in the past. He kept showing up in his business the way he thought he had to be:

- **Directive** – Otherwise people "wouldn't know what they were doing or what needed to be achieved, right?"
- **Untouchable** – Never displaying when he wasn't sure about something, or needed input from someone else with more knowledge, as "this is a sign of weakness, right?"
- **Modeling Busyness** – Always on a device, always accessible, with the mantra, "I need to always be available to everyone, right?"
- **Blinkered** – Always thinking he had the answers and not prepared to listen to the *juniors* in his team. "They know nothing, right?"

Notice what this behavior spells? Remember, the BS we have, (Blind Spots, Beliefs Systems, Bullsh*t), these created the patterns of response and way of being for Dean, until he worked with us. There is no blame, shame, guilt, or judgement in this recognition, as these were just patterns that Dean developed throughout his life and career.

He showed up in his business the way he *thought* he had to (like so many of the leaders we work with). He was too focused on always having the answers and being *available*, yet he was also missing the invaluable opportunities to connect, collaborate, and lead authentically.

It was an absolute privilege and joy to work with Dean and give him the tools to become more of an Authentic Leader. To embrace his incredible strengths and put in place the specific strategies in this book, and more, to inspire and influence his team in a much more successful way.

We began with the same strategies shared in this book. They work, *when* you put them into action, *consistently!* These actions then become your activity; familiar, powerful things that are integrated into your everyday life, that elevate your clarity, confidence and certainty, even more.

When you BE congruent with your whole self, and DO these strategies consistently, you will then HAVE the impact and influence your desire.

HAVE – The Ripple Effect Of Authenticity

What you ultimately HAVE as an Authentic Leader is never about just external results. It is about building sustainable impact.

- You *HAVE* the roadmap forward
- You *HAVE* the trust of your people
- You *HAVE* the loyalty of those who choose to follow you
- You *HAVE* the influence to inspire change, the resilience to navigate challenges, and the results that don't burn you out, but build you up.

Authenticity is not a finish line that you cross once. It's the outcome of consistently choosing to BE authentic, DO authenticity, and HAVE authentic moments.

This has a natural ripple effect on the level of trust you have in yourself, the level of belief you have in yourself, the level of certainty you have in your resourcefulness. This then dribbles, flows, or cascades (you get to choose), into your team and the people around you where levels of trust, impact, and sustainable results explode even more.

When you live this sequence fully, what you HAVE is bigger than success, it's legacy. The *thing* that outlasts you. The impact that still happens even when you are not around. The contributions you have made, the visions you have embellished, the innovation you have disrupted, that leaves an indelible mark of others. That catapults humanity to a different place, that exudes realness, truth and compassion in who you BE, and what you leave behind.

Authentic leaders understand that their legacy will be defined not only by what they achieve but by *how they achieve it*. The *how* cannot be done without the BEing first.

Masks And Authentic Leadership

One of the greatest barriers to BEing, DOing, and HAVEing authenticity is the habit of wearing masks.

As you can see in the image on the cover of this influential book, the design itself tells a story:

The infinity circle represents the continuous flow of past, present, and future, reminding us that authenticity is an ever-evolving journey of integration, not perfection.

At the centre lies a heart, symbolising that Authentic Leadership begins and ends with compassion, courage, and connection.

The mask serves as a bold reminder that it's not something to wear, but something to *remove*.

A mask can be a powerful projection used to impress others, or a powerful protection used to hide behind. Either way, a mask distances you from your true self, and limits the impact you can have.

Leaders often slip different masks on to fit expectations, avoid criticism, or project a polished version of themselves.

These masks are often in place when the Toxic Ten show up, and indicate a moment when you can shift those past patterns to instead embrace the true YOU! These masks may help you blend in, but *they cost you* your power, your presence, and your connection, with yourself first and then with others.

When you wear a mask, you block others from seeing the real you, and in turn, *you rob yourself of the freedom* of being seen, accepted, and trusted.

Authentic Leadership *demands* that you take the mask off, even when it feels uncomfortable. True influence comes not from perfection, but from showing up as your true self, no matter what.

The moment you drop the mask, you create a space where others feel safe to do the same, and that's when teams, relationships, and organizations begin to thrive. If you want to truly HAVE authenticity, you must first be willing to let go of the performance and stand in the truth of who you genuinely are.

This is our invitation to you: Lead with your whole heart, unmasked and fully present, where your true power and influence reside.

Living Beyond The Mask: Your Authentic Legacy

Authentic Leadership isn't something you switch on when it's convenient. It's not a role, a tactic, or a performance. It's who you are; fully, consistently, and unapologetically.

When you BE authentic, DO in alignment with that being, and embrace the ripple effect of what you HAVE, you step into a leadership presence that is unstoppable, magnetic, and transformative.

Every choice you make, every action you take, and every connection you foster becomes a reflection of the real you. The more you shed masks, the clearer your influence becomes. The more you embody your authentic self, the more others feel safe to step into their authenticity. This is where true leadership lives: in courage, clarity, and connection.

You've learned the framework, tools, and practices and you've seen the impact they create. Now it's time for you to choose what comes next. Choose to follow through and take your Authentic Leadership to the next level. Not just to be a leader who achieves results, but to be a leader whose presence, influence, and legacy elevates everyone and everything around you.

The world doesn't need another leader who performs the way they think they *should* be performing. The world needs YOU! Fully seen, fully real, fully alive, and only YOU can BE this unique version of you!

Then and only then, can you create *high-performing teams* as an Authentic Leader.

Creating High-Performing Teams Through Authentic Leadership

Stepping into this section, we now identify the importance of the HAVE in the BE - DO - HAVE model in your leadership.

But what does it really mean to HAVE a high-performing team?

Before you get scared or think, *I just want to have a good team that produces some good stuff,* remember that it takes more work to create an average, mediocre, beige team, than it does to create a High-Performing one.

After all, no Leader is a Leader without a team. But let's be crystal clear, this does *not* mean you have a group of people in your team who simply do what you tell them. Authentic Leadership is not dictatorship. Authentic Leadership is leading yourself first, setting the standards internally, and then inspiring those around you to rise to that same level.

Nowhere is this better illustrated than in the New Zealand All Blacks, the world's most successful rugby team. Their team culture is a masterclass in Authentic Leadership and high-performance.

The All Blacks embody three uncompromising truths:

- High performance starts from within
- Standards must be self-imposed, not externally policed
- Leadership works best when the team takes the lead.

In other words, lead yourself, raise your standards, and then trust your team to rise with you. Until you know what you truly want to HAVE in your life, in your leadership, and in your team, you're drifting through someone else's agenda. Drifting to other people's playbook and allowing yourself to be reactive, not pro-active.

Drifting leaders don't build high-performing teams. Drifting leaders get tossed around by external factors.

Clarity is the antidote. Without it, you're reacting to whatever comes at you, instead of driving the play yourself. The shift from drifting to deliberate starts when you choose the target.

You can't hit a target that you haven't set. If you want to HAVE something in your career, leadership, or life, then you must be clear on exactly what that is. What it looks like, sounds like, and feels like.

The Raw Truth About High-Performing Teams

Whenever we step into an organization, we ask the leaders this question: "Who here has a high-performing team?"

Usually, 80% or more shoot their hands up. Then we ask them to check in and clarify a few things:

- Do you *always* have clear, courageous conversations with candor?
- Do you *immediately* call out mistakes and celebrate the learnings?
- Do you *constantly* pursue personal and professional growth together?
- Does *every* team member take full ownership and accountability for their actions, at all times?

- Do you have *laser-focused, distraction-free meetings* with specific outcomes?

By the end of that line of questioning, *all* the hands in the room have dropped. Even though most leaders want to believe they're leading a high-performing team, very few actually are.

High-performing teams are *not* built on wishful thinking, sugar coating problems, use of leadership focussed one-liners as motivators or ignoring poor behaviors.

High-performing teams *are* built on *consistent, uncompromising standards and behaviors.*

The DNA Of A High-Performing Team

Christine

High-performing teams don't happen by accident. They're not born from luck or talent alone, nor the presence of one charismatic leader. They are forged in the fire of intention, built through commitment, and strengthened by consistent practice.

A true high-performing team is about showing up in the highs, the lows, the celebrations, the tough times, and everything in between, together.

The best team I have ever been part of was our Exercise Science Department at WelTec, in Wellington, New Zealand. On paper, we were a motley crew. Different backgrounds, different strengths, flaws, quirks, and brilliance.

In reality, we were a force. A sensational unit. A team that connected, trusted, and had each other's backs, no matter what.

Even now, as I sit here sipping my coffee and smiling at the memories, I can feel it. The barbeques, the coffees (and a few cheeky beverages), the social times, the mountain biking, the literal and metaphorical hills we climbed, the conversations filled with raw candor, the early mornings and the late nights. We worked hard, we played hard, and we held ourselves to a standard that others simply couldn't understand.

We had unwritten rules and our own culture of excellence. We respected each other deeply. We celebrated wins, we called each other out with honesty and care, and we kept each other accountable. We didn't need a handbook, we simply lived the values of authenticity, respect, and unity.

And people noticed. Our students respected us. Our industry admired us, because we consistently produced graduates of the highest caliber. Fellow staff admired us too, though some despised us. Those who were inauthentic tried to belittle what we had. Those with hidden agendas ridiculed us for having fun, for playing games, for finishing an entire year's workload ahead of everyone else. But we knew the truth.

Our ability to perform came not in spite of our culture, but *because* of it.

Our team's strength wasn't just professional, it was deeply personal. I'll never forget the day my dad passed away and then what it was like to attend his funeral. My entire team restructured the student timetable for that day, got in cars, and drove two hours to stand with me and my whānau (family). That wasn't just respect, that was love. That was solidarity. That was what it means to truly be there for one another.

We laughed, we cried, we nudged each other forward when needed, we hugged, we supported, we played, and sometimes we simply sat in silence, knowing words weren't required. We understood each other. We valued each other. We stretched and grew because of each other.

That is what a high-performing team is. Not a group of perfect individuals, but a collection of authentic, committed, connected humans who unite around a shared purpose, hold each other accountable, and lift one another to heights none could ever reach alone.

We weren't just colleagues. We were family. We were a Dream Team!

For you to get an insider's look at what a highly effective team is about, here are the 7 Pillars of a High-Performing Team - what they *have*, what they *do*, and what it *feels* like, when you are part of one:

1. Clear And Courageous Communication

High-performing teams thrive on communication that is direct, concise, and meaningful. There is no smoke, no mirrors, and no second-guessing. Every member speaks with candor rather than ego, and every voice matters. Authentic Leadership is not about achieving agreement or deferring to hierarchy. It is about speaking up and, equally important, listening with the intent to understand, not merely to respond.

Clear, courageous communication requires asking questions that clarify and probe deeper, rather than accepting the first comment at face value. It involves confronting tough conversations head-on and mastering the art of holding courageous discussions with ease. When leaders model these skills, they empower their teams to embrace and internalize them.

When communication is transparent and intentional, wasted energy on office politics, misinterpretations, and gossip disappears. Expectations are clearly understood, accountability is built, and teams move forward with confidence and purpose.

2. Growth Through CANI Feedback (Constant And Never-ending Improvement)

Feedback doesn't need to be awkward, avoided, or wrapped in meaningless platitudes that sugar-coat the truth. Feedback is a *lifeline*. A chance to reflect, listen, weigh things up, analyse, decide, and choose what to change. It gives both you and others the opportunity to identify specific actions and behaviors that can be repeated, and those that can be enhanced even more.

When used intentionally, feedback becomes one of the most powerful tools an Authentic Leader has to build trust, growth, and psychological safety.

The *CANI Feedback Method* is grounded in the psychology of how humans best receive information and is inspired by the Japanese philosophy of *Kaizen* which champions continuous, incremental growth. Based on global research from the Corporate Leadership Council involving more than 19,000 people across industries, we know that when leaders focus on strengths and what's going well, productivity increases by over 36%. When they focus on enhancing those strengths - what can be done "even better" - productivity can rise by over 62%.[42]

When attention is directed toward weaknesses, limitations, or *fixing* what's wrong, productivity drops by more than 26%. This evidence reinforces what we intuitively know as Authentic Leaders: People grow faster and perform better when their strengths are seen, valued, and built upon.

When Authentic Leaders give feedback using the *CANI method*, every conversation follows a clear structure so that it aligns with intention, lands with purpose, and creates progress, not defensiveness. It focuses on observable behaviors and actions, not emotions or personal traits.

The strategy is simple, specific, and powerful:

Step 1: *Identify what was good.* Be genuine, clear, and specific, not vague, general or flippant. Begin with: "What was good about this was..." and highlight exactly what you want repeated again.

Step 2: *Identify what will make it even better.* Frame this in the future tense using: "What will make this even better is..." to clarify behaviors or actions that would elevate their performance next time. Always state what you *do want*, not what you don't want.

Step 3: *End with the one best thing.* Finish on a high note: "The best thing about this was..." This reinforces what's working and leaves the person feeling confident and inspired to grow.

---

[42] Imai M. Kaizen: *The Key to Japan's Competitive Success.* New York: McGraw-Hill; 1986.

You must use these phrases to begin each section. They are crafted to spark curiosity and openness. The number of 'things' you recognize in Step 1 must be more than in Step 2. That is, if you have two things you want to include in *Make this even better* (Step 2) then you must have three behaviors or actions in Step 1 that you are reinforcing.

If you have a list of 10 things, don't go there! People cannot absorb that many. Narrow your focus, and pick your top one-to-three priorities to get the biggest impact. Keep it simple and intentional.

Real change comes from clarity, not quantity.

Remember, we all, individually, get to choose what feedback we take on board as well. As my coach once told me, "Try feedback on like a jacket; decide what you'll keep and what you'll release." Implementing feedback is a personal responsibility; receiving it is an act of courage. It's about choosing what to take on board and having the humility to face the harder truths that stretch us toward our potential.

Imagine a team where feedback is welcomed, not feared. Where mistakes are seen as opportunities, not personal attacks. Where the culture proudly screams: "We're in this to grow together!"

That is *CANI in action*, the heartbeat of constant, authentic, and never-ending improvement.

3. Structured, Purpose-Driven Meetings And Collaborations

High-performing teams avoid meetings that are mere talking shops or opinion fests.

Instead, every interaction, meeting, or huddle is sharp, structured, and outcome-driven. Every participant arrives prepared, knowing the purpose, the agenda, and their role. The result is clear: Everyone leaves knowing exactly who is responsible for what, by when, and to what extent.

Structured collaboration is about eliminating wasted energy and creating laser-focused momentum. Beyond meetings, it extends to prioritizing team goals over personal objectives. Authentic Leaders know that ego must never drive the agenda: Mission drives the agenda. Sometimes leaders and team members need to defer personal glory to elevate collective success. This is the high-performing team understanding that personal brilliance only matters when it fuels the team's impact.

In essence, team members ask themselves, *Who do I need to* BE and *What can I* DO *to make the team better?* rather than, *How can the team make me look good?* This mindset builds unity, loyalty, and a purpose greater than any single individual.

4. Radical Accountability And Rapid Recovery

High-performing teams operate *above the line*, where accountability is a catalyst for growth, trust, and performance, rather than a tool for punishment. Each member owns their decisions, actions (behavior), and results, leaving no room for blame, excuses, or victimhood. We always aim for staying *above-the-line* and setting this standard for our teams.

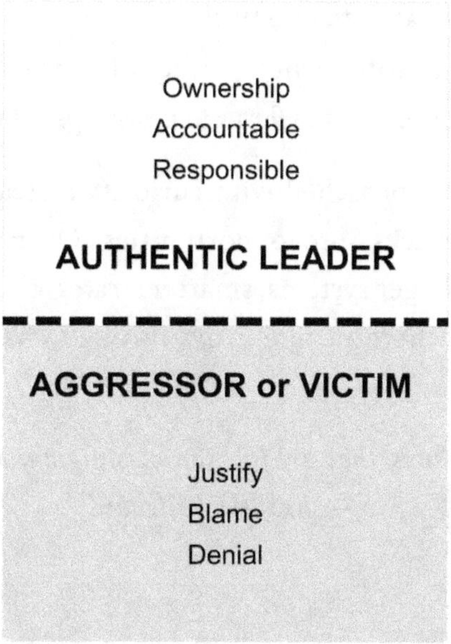

Ownership
Accountable
Responsible

AUTHENTIC LEADER

- - - - - - - - - - - -

AGGRESSOR or VICTIM

Justify
Blame
Denial

Figure 2: Above And Below The Line Leadership

Falling below the line, blaming, finger-pointing, justifying, or excuse-making, is inevitable at times, but Authentic Leaders notice, pause, and choose again, using our NPC Method. Then, you can quickly realign and shift into accountability, ownership and responsibility.

The language of accountability shifts from *But they... (looking towards anyone to blame other than myself)*, to; *What can I do differently?* or *What can I learn from this?* or *Where else in my life am I avoiding accountability?*

When accountability becomes radical ownership, mistakes cease to be failures and become progress points. Challenges are solved faster, trust deepens, and momentum compounds.

This philosophy extends to recovering quickly from mistakes. In psychologically safe environments, errors aren't hidden or punished, they are acknowledged openly, owned swiftly, and resolved collaboratively. One powerful way to embed this mindset is through a regular ritual of holding a monthly *mistake party*.

Each month bring your team together to:

- Reflect on what didn't go well
- Identify the lesson learned (without blame or judgment)
- Ask: *What would it take for us to never repeat this mistake again?*

When mistakes are approached with curiosity instead of criticism, they transform from setbacks into opportunities. Over time, these shared learnings lead to stronger systems, smarter strategies, and a more resilient team culture. One where people grow through challenges rather than shrink from them.

Mistakes are not failures, they are fuel for learning, innovation, and growth.
—Elizabeth Pritchard

5. Trust, Vulnerability, And Psychological Safety

Trust is the foundation of high-performing teams. It is earned, nurtured, and fiercely protected. Authentic Leaders cultivate an environment where teammates know they will follow through, support one another, and operate without suspicion or hidden agendas.

Trust operates at two levels:

- **Personal trust**: *I know you'll do what you say you'll do.*
- **Collective trust**: *I know we can count on each other to win together.*

When both are present, high performance is inevitable.

Trust flourishes alongside *radical vulnerability*. Teams declare successes and failures openly, understanding that vulnerability is a strength, not a weakness. Authentic Leaders model this *first*, admitting when they don't know something, when they make mistakes, or when they need help. Vulnerability normalizes authenticity, fosters psychological safety, and encourages shared ownership of growth and innovation.

Psychological safety is the bedrock of all high-performing teams. Without it, trust crumbles, candor disappears, and progress stalls. With it, individuals feel safe to challenge assumptions, share bold ideas, admit mistakes, ask for help, and embrace accountability.

Every other element of high performance - feedback, collaboration, innovation - relies on this foundation.

6. Unshakable Support And Team Cohesion

High-performing teams operate with a *We not Me* mentality. Success isn't about individual glory, it's about collective achievement. When one person stumbles, others step in *without hesitation*. There is a fierce, unwavering loyalty that says, "I've got your back, always."

This kind of support builds unshakable confidence, enabling everyone to take smart risks and stretch beyond their comfort zones, knowing they won't fall alone. It goes far beyond simple teamwork. In these teams, people show up for each other *consistently*, not just when it's convenient. They actively seek ways to lift one another, share knowledge, and amplify each other's strengths.

Authentic Leaders set the tone by modeling this behavior. They celebrate wins openly, share burdens willingly, and encourage team members to ask for help when needed. They discourage silent suffering and create a culture where reaching out for support is seen as a sign of strength, not weakness.

The message is clear: "We rise together, or we don't rise at all."

When support is this strong, *trust deepens, resilience multiplies,* and high performance becomes sustainable. Teams move *further, faster,* solving problems creatively and *recovering quickly* from setbacks because no one is carrying the weight alone.

This level of connection transforms a group of talented individuals into a *cohesive, unstoppable unit.* It is in these moments that teams stop being just teams and start becoming *families, not by blood, but by choice,* and bonded by a shared purpose and unwavering commitment to each other's success.

7. Energy, Celebration, And Joy

High performance is fueled not just by effort and discipline but by fun, laughter, and strategic breaks. Joy energizes, sparks creativity, strengthens bonds, and signals psychological safety. Whether through light-hearted activities in the office or scheduled recovery pauses, teams that embrace fun maintain focus, innovation, and connection.

Celebrating wins and continuous learning is equally vital. Recognition, whether for successes, efforts, or lessons learned, reinforces behaviors, strengthens culture, and builds momentum. Celebrating progress, effort and courage, rather than waiting for perfect outcomes, ensures that teams remain motivated, innovative, and aligned with their purpose.

Fun, laughter, and celebration are not distractions, they are accelerators. They are motivators. They are essential! Teams that can laugh together innovate together. They thrive not only on achievement but on the collective joy of creating something meaningful.

These seven pillars are more than ideas; they are the *living heartbeat of high-performing teams.* When they are present, work becomes more than just tasks; it transforms into a shared mission built on trust, purpose, and collective growth.

High performance doesn't happen by chance. It's built *intentionally* with one conversation, one decision, one action at a time. As you reflect on these pillars, ask yourself: Which are thriving in your team, and which need attention? Start small, focus on one, and build from there. When a team lives these principles, they don't just perform, they *elevate,* creating a space where people and results can truly soar.

Be A REAL Model, Not A Role Model

You can't expect your team to show behaviors that you don't live by yourself. Words alone aren't enough. Teams *mirror what you do, not what you say.*

Authentic Leaders cannot aim to just be role models. They must become *REAL models.* They don't perform leadership for applause, external validation, or optics, they *embody* authenticity. In every interaction, every conversation, every decision, every day.

Being a *REAL model* means showing up consistently with integrity, courage, and authenticity. It means holding yourself accountable, celebrating wins, admitting mistakes, and supporting others, even when it's hard or at some cost to your own goal achievement timeline.

When leaders live their values visibly and deliberately, the team naturally aligns, trusts, and rises to that standard.

Authenticity is contagious. Your actions set the culture, so BE the example you want your team to follow. That's why Authentic Leaders are *REAL models!* They don't *perform* leadership for the crowd, they *are* the leader; every single day, in every single way, with every single person.

2X vs. 10X Teams

If you've become complacent or comfortable in your leadership, let this statement slap you awake: *An ineffective team takes more energy to manage than a high-performing one.*

Why? Because an average team operates in 2X mode. You're doing more of the same work with the same outdated mindset; twice the effort, twice the hustle, twice the grind, twice the frustration.

And for what? Twice the Bullsh*t.

Now consider this: The 10X concept completely transforms the game. As Sullivan & Hardy explain, building a 10X team is not about working harder, it's about thinking totally differently. A 10X team operates at a level of flow, creativity, trust, and alignment that makes the work feel easier, not heavier. Energy is multiplied, not drained. Ideas are generated faster, decisions are smarter, and execution becomes smoother.[43]

High-performing teams are not harder to lead, they're easier.

The catch?

You need the *courage* to build one. You must let go of outdated habits and beliefs, invest in psychological safety, revolutionary vulnerability, and radical accountability, and intentionally cultivate alignment, trust, and shared purpose.

---

[43] Sullivan D, Hardy B. *10x is easier than 2x: How world-class entrepreneurs achieve more by doing less.* New York: Hay House; 2023.

When you commit to 10X thinking, you stop managing mediocrity and start unlocking genius. Every person shows up fully. Every process is streamlined. Every interaction compounds energy instead of draining it.

Authentic Leadership becomes a multiplier, not a burden, and suddenly, achieving extraordinary results feels not just possible, but inevitable.

Run Your Business Like A Sports Team

Christine

There was a time in my business journey when I felt completely out of sync.

I was working hard, following all the *rules* of how to run a company, and trying to fit into a mold of what a *good* CEO should look like. I read the books, attended the conferences, and copied the methods of other leaders who seemed to have it all figured out.

The problem? It felt unnatural. Forced. And deep down, I knew it wasn't working.

One day with the help of my 10x community, I had a moment of clarity:

> *I already know how to lead a high-performing team. I've done it in many sports. Why am I not applying those same principles to my business?*

That insight shifted everything. From that point on, I stopped trying to run my business the *traditional* way and started running it the way I knew best: Like a sports team.

This wasn't just a mindset change, it was the culmination of everything we have written in this Authentic Leadership playbook.

All the work on emotional agility, self-awareness, influence, and building your team of co-elevators led to this moment. Every principle, every exercise, every insight, every mindset choice was designed to help you perform at your peak while staying true to who you are.

Running your business like a sports team means:

- **Clarity of roles and responsibilities:** Everyone knows their position, their purpose, and how they contribute to the overall game plan.
- **Trust and accountability:** Like elite athletes, your team thrives when people are accountable to each other, lifting each other up, challenging each other, having each others' back, and keeping each other honest.
- **Consistency in training and preparation:** Peak performance doesn't happen by chance. It comes from deliberate, consistent effort, reflection, and feedback.
- **Celebrating the wins and learning from the losses:** Every game, every project, every quarter is an opportunity to grow, refine, and excel *together*.

When you run your business like a sports team, you stop trying to do everything yourself, and you start leveraging the strengths of your team. You build a culture where high performance and authenticity are inseparable. Where resilience, focus, and joy coexist. Where you - and your team - show up fully and consistently, every single day.

This is more than leadership. This is Authentic Leadership that lasts. Leadership that elevates the people around you and your business. Your playbook is ready. The team is ready. It's time to take the field and play *full out.*

The Internal Shift

The first step wasn't about systems or structures. It wasn't even about my team. It was about me.

To lead like a coach, I first had to get out of my own way. I call this dealing with *my BS.*

- **Belief Systems:** The stories I'd been told and my beliefs about what leadership *should* look like.

- **Blind Spots:** The things I didn't know I didn't know; *assumptions* I hadn't challenged.
- **Bullsh*t:** The *excuses, self-doubt,* and *fear* that kept me playing small.

Once I stripped those away, I could see clearly. I stopped pretending to be someone else's version of a CEO and stepped fully into my own Authentic Leadership style.

This was the pivotal mindset shift that allowed everything else to fall into place.

Let People Be Their Genius

On any sports team, every player has a defined role. The goalie isn't expected to score goals. The striker isn't asked to defend the net. Yet in business, we often do the opposite. We place people in roles that don't fit them, or we expect them to be good at everything, and then wonder why performance suffers.

My job as a leader became clear:

Identify each person's unique genius and create space for them to fully own it.

When people are working in their zone of genius, they light up. They're motivated, inspired, productive, and deeply engaged. When they're not, frustration builds for them and for everyone around them.

Building A Culture Of Open Communication

High-performing sports teams have one thing in common: Constant, clear, and candid communication. When you're on the court, the turf, the field, the water, or the track, there's no time for confusion or second-guessing. You call the play, you trust your teammates, and you move as one.

I brought this same principle into my business. It wasn't about more meetings, it was about *better conversations:*

- Quick, direct updates instead of long-winded discussions.
- Open, honest feedback with no hidden agendas.
- Future-focused communication: Anticipating challenges, thinking ahead, and *passing the ball* to where it *needs* to go, not just where it is now.

This created a sense of trust and flow. Everyone knew where they stood, what was expected, and how their role connected to the whole.

Handling Underperformance

Not every player shows up at their best every day, in sport or business.

When performance slipped, I didn't jump to blame. Instead, I approached it like a coach:

1. **Call it early** - Don't let small issues grow into big ones.
2. **Understand their reality** - Ask what's going on before assuming the worst.
3. **Reset the standards** - Be clear about the standards required to stay in the *starting lineup.*

If someone consistently couldn't meet the standards, even after support and honest conversations, it became a matter of can do, will do, team fit. It didn't mean they were a bad person; it just meant they were in the wrong position, or maybe even the wrong team.

The Results

When we truly embraced this sports team approach, the transformation was remarkable.

- The team became *happier, more confident, and more connected.*
- Communication was smoother, faster, and clearer.

- Creativity and innovation skyrocketed.
- Productivity doubled.
- And yes, *our revenue doubled too.*

Even more powerful was the ripple effect. Clients felt the shift. The energy of a united, high-performing team extended outward, creating a *tenfold increase in external impact.*

How To Run Your Business Like A Sports Team

Here are the core practices I followed to create this shift:

- **Start with mindset.** Get out of your own way and lead authentically by showing up as your true self and creating space for others to do the same.
- **Define clear roles and expectations.** Everyone needs to know their position and what success looks like.
- **Play to strengths.** Identify each team member's genius and let them shine.
- **Communicate constantly and candidly.** Keep it open, direct, and future-focused.
- **Address issues early.** Have courageous conversations before problems grow.
- **Set and protect team standards.** High performance comes from shared accountability.
- **Focus on the team, not individuals.** No one wins alone; success is *always* collective.

The Big Lesson

At the heart of this approach is a simple truth: *When everyone owns their position and plays it well, the whole team wins.*

As a leader, your role isn't to do everything or know everything. It's to create the conditions where every person can bring their best self to the arena, and trust that their teammates will do the same.

When that happens, business stops feeling like a grind and starts feeling like a game worth playing.

Now It's Your Turn

Before you rush off and demand a *high-performing team*, pause and ask yourself:

- What do I truly *want* for this team?
- What does success *look, sound, and feel like?*
- Who do I need to *be* to lead them there?
- What genius do I get to *invite, hire, or collaborate* with?

Remember: You cannot have a high-performing team without first being a high-performing leader. It starts with YOU.

Authentic Leadership is never about control, it's about creation. It's not about telling people what to do, but *showing* them who to *be*. It's not about being "good enough," but knowing you already are enough and igniting greatness.

So here's the challenge: Stop settling for beige. Stop managing mediocrity. Step up and raise your standards. Show up as the leader who naturally attracts, builds, and sustains a truly high-performing team.

Because the world doesn't need more average teams, it needs Authentic Leaders brave enough to be *extraordinary*. Leaders who embody excellence, inspire trust, and create an unstoppable team culture where potential is unlocked, energy is multiplied, and every success compounds.

High-performing teams don't happen by accident. They happen because you choose to BE the leader they deserve.

BE the leader who embodies courage, clarity, and authenticity. DO the behaviors that inspire, empower, and elevate your team, and then you will HAVE the high-performing team you want.

Chapter Takeaways:

BE Before You HAVE – Authentic impact begins with who you are and how you show up consistently.

Authenticity First – When you lead from truth, trust and influence naturally follow. The ripple effect is huge.

Drop the Masks – Show up fully and lead from your real self, not your role. Drop the façade and expectations of what you think you *should* be doing.

Consistency Builds Credibility – Repeated authentic action builds trust and credibility faster than words ever can.

Trust and Influence – People follow leaders who are real, not perfect. Authenticity is a magnetic force for good.

Lead by Example – Teams mirror who you are *BEing*, not what you are *DOing*. Model the mindset, decision making, and responses you want to see in them.

High Performance Starts Within – Strong teams are built by leaders who self-regulate, communicate, and stay grounded in the present.

Courageous Communication – Honest, clear dialogue with candor, drives connection and collective success.

Strengths-Based Feedback – Focusing on strengths builds engagement, motivation, and growth. Use the CANI strategy to take yourself and your team to the next level.

Play to Strengths – Focus on strengths, not limitations. Empower people to lead from their zone of genius and see the results. Tell them what you *do* want. **Run Your Business Like A Sports Team** – Clarify their strengths, hold them accountable, and encourage ownership of their genius. This turns teams into champions.

Radical Accountability – Own your mistakes boldly. Learn from them quickly. Step above the line with responsibility and take intentional action.

Stop Managing Mediocrity – Set high standards, model excellence, and be the Authentic Leader your team deserves.

Leading Forward:

What is the one daring, uncompromising leap you are taking right now that will catapult everything you've learned in this book into the extraordinary?

This is your moment to fully step into the next-level version of yourself as an Authentic Leader: fearing less, being unstoppable, and owning your magnificence. Choose it, commit to it consistently, and let it ignite a lifetime of clarity, confidence, and impact that far exceeds anything you have ever imagined.

CHAPTER 10

The Next-Level Authentic Leader

"The privilege of a lifetime is to become who you truly are."
—Carl Yung

Authentic Leadership is not a final stop, but an ever-evolving journey of alignment and truth. This is the moment where everything converges; where who you BE, what you DO, and what you HAVE, fuse together into a force that creates lasting impact, trust, and fulfillment.

Strategic leadership is the next expression of this journey: Channeling your authenticity to shape a powerful vision, make bold decisions, and align your team toward long-term impact.

It's more than theory: It's your call to rise, to step fully into your power, to lead with unwavering courage, and to shape a legacy that boldly reflects your deepest values and your greatest vision.

The BE → DO → HAVE Legacy Of Authentic Leadership

Authentic Leadership is not built in moments of convenience. Rather, it is forged in the courageous choice to live in alignment with who you are BEing, what you DO, and the legacy you HAVE to leave behind.

In Section One, BE, we explored the foundation. You discovered that leadership begins within cultivating self-awareness, emotional regulation, psychological capital, and agency. It's not about ego, perfection, or approval. It's about showing up with curiosity, compassion, and integrity. When you anchor into who you truly are, you become the steady presence others trust and follow.

In Section Two, DO, we moved into action. Here, authenticity takes form through mindset, language, agency, and courageous choices. You now hold the tools to set boundaries, have the conversations that matter, manage your energy, and make decisions with clarity and conviction. Leadership becomes a living practice where who you are, shapes what you do.

In Section Three, HAVE, we elevated it into impact. Authentic Leadership produces outcomes that matter; health, wealth, trust, team excellence, and fulfillment. By aligning BEing and DOing with purpose, you create results that endure. Sustainability, self-care, and continuous growth keep you fueled, while your integrity multiplies influence across every life you touch.

And now, here you stand. You have journeyed through the methods, tools, and mindset shifts that empower you to BE an Authentic Leader. The question is, how do you keep this alive? How do you stretch into the next level of your Authentic Leadership and sustain the breakthroughs you've already made?

This is your invitation. Ask the bold questions. Keep choosing courage over comfort. Lead with integrity, compassion, and fire. Because when you live the BE → DO → HAVE model, you don't just lead, you ignite movements, transform cultures, and carve a legacy that will outlast you.

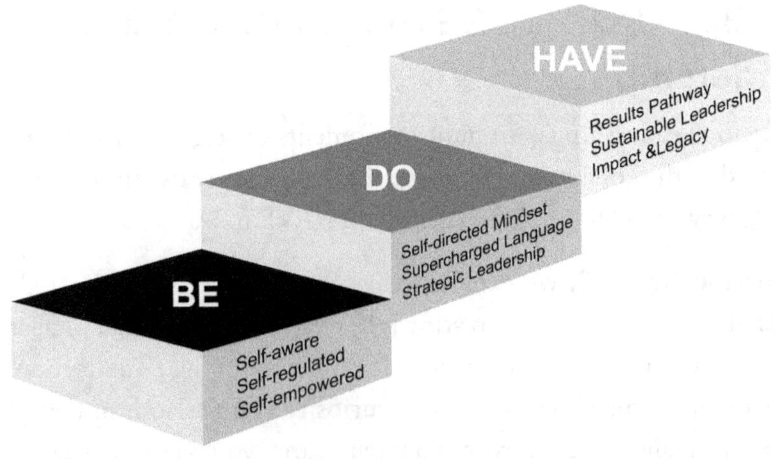

Figure 3: Be - Do - Have Model

First, Remember That You Already Are Enough

Everything you need to *BE* an Authentic Leader is already inside you.

This book has never been a manual; *it's a mirror.* A reflection of your fire, your calling, your untapped potential.

You are already the leader you've been searching for. The only difference now is this: You consciously hold the tools to unleash what has always been within.

This Authentic Leadership Playbook, has handed you the strategies, the processes, and the tools to bust through the BS, annihilate the Toxic Ten, and practice being your authentic self.

Every day, in every conversation, every challenge, and every choice, you get to choose what that is for you.

This is about taking one bold, consistent step forward, every day, until it becomes who you are at the deepest level of your being. You now have the tools and strategies to show up every day, consciously, purposefully, intentionally, and powerfully!

One thing is a must: You *must* take action and build the muscle of being authentic. Knowledge without action is nothing. Whether you formally lead others or not, we implore you to keep putting this information into deliberate, intentional action. Keep taking consistent, daily action that will yield the results, and create the legacy of your impact.

Tastes Of Success: Fuel Your Next Move

Experiencing tastes of success is a powerful way to reinforce progress and build momentum. By intentionally celebrating wins, big or small, Authentic Leaders continue to embed new habits, strengthen confidence, and signal to themselves and their teams that their efforts are making a difference.

Each celebration becomes an opportunity not just to acknowledge effort and achievement, but to choose the next tiny tweak, the next deliberate action, that elevates performance and takes habits to the next level. In this way, recognition and reflection fuel continuous growth, turning moments of success into lasting impact.

Resistance Revealed: Spotting Your Inner Saboteur

When you step into next-level leadership to pursue a higher potential, you will encounter resistance. Steven Pressfield in his book *The War of Art* calls this the enemy within; a force that manifests as procrastination, self-doubt, fear, rationalization, or distraction.[44] Resistance doesn't just appear externally (the sick parent, the injured child, the financial challenge), it rises from within, whenever we attempt to grow, stretch, or act boldly.

Resistance is the mind's way of protecting the status quo, keeping you safe in familiar patterns, and avoiding the discomfort of transformation. The more meaningful and aligned your next step, the louder resistance becomes.

Recognizing resistance is the first step in overcoming it. Naming it for what it is - a predictable, internal saboteur - gives it less power over your choices. Authentic Leaders can anticipate that whenever they stretch beyond previous limits, the enemy within will surface.

Resistance might look like delaying a courageous conversation, overthinking a decision, or questioning your ability to lead authentically. But remember, resistance is *not* a signal to stop, it's a sign that you are *stepping into growth.*

---

[44] Pressfield S. *The war of art: Break through the blocks and win your inner creative battles.* New York (NY): Warner Books; 2002.

Overcoming resistance requires deliberate action. Pressfield reminds us that the antidote is simple but not easy: *Do your work anyway*. Authentic Leaders can overcome internal resistance by following through with the strategies we have shared:

- Showing up consistently
- Breaking tasks into small, achievable steps
- Asking for help
- Embracing accountability
- Celebrating micro-wins along the way

Each act of courage weakens resistance's grip, reinforces agency, and proves that discomfort is not an obstacle, but a companion to growth. Ultimately, confronting resistance becomes a practice in self-mastery, resilience, and leading self authentically.

Gay Hendricks in *The Big Leap*, describes a similar phenomenon, the Upper Limit Problem. This is where we unconsciously sabotage ourselves when we reach new heights of success, love, or abundance because it feels unfamiliar or threatening. Together, these frameworks reveal that the enemy is often within, a psychological barrier that both warns and restrains us.[45]

Overcoming this barrier requires awareness, deliberate action (*The STOP Technique)*, and the courage to step into discomfort *repeatedly*. This turns resistance and upper-limit alerts into signals of growth rather than barriers to progress.

---

[45] Hendricks G. *The big leap: Conquer your hidden fear and take life to the next level.* New York (NY): HarperOne; 2009.

Lead Without Limits: Your Next-Level Invitation

This is your moment. Your invitation is simple: Do the work on yourself with urgency.

Do it NOW. Not tomorrow, not when it's convenient. NOW.

Write down the strategies. Practice them with relentless, high-energy commitment. Remember, you get to choose your state, you set your mindset, you create the dialogue within. That dialogue shapes who you BE, what you DO, and ultimately, what you HAVE.

You get to choose: Stay stuck in the funk of outdated leadership? Or break through the BS, claim your truth, and lead with authenticity?

The choice is yours, and so are the consequences.

You may not always be liked, you may not always be popular, but popularity is not the measure of Authentic Leadership. When you lead with integrity, courage, and purpose, you magnetize the right people. Your energy becomes the gravity that pulls in those who are ready to build, to grow, and to rise alongside you.

So ask yourself: "When is NOW a good time to start?" The answer has always been the same - NOW. Here. In *this* moment. This is where Authentic Leadership comes alive.

When You Think You've Failed, You Are Actually Winning

When the outcome isn't what you anticipated, it's easy to perceive failure. But what if it's actually perfect for this moment of growth? What if this is the perfect opportunity to learn something about yourself, to explore something that has been hidden, or to tweak something you have not yet had the opportunity to do?

Remember, when you notice something that initially may be seen as a failure, Authentic Leaders practice no blame, no shame, no guilt, no judgment, and turn stumbles into opportunities for growth.

This is a fantastic place to use the NPC method (Notice → Pause → Choose Again) which offers a structured way to reset. Notice what happened, pause to step out of reactive patterns, and choose the next action intentionally. What feels like a failure becomes feedback, a signal guiding you toward learning, adaptation, and alignment with your values.

By reframing outcomes this way, Authentic Leaders reclaim agency, maintain clarity, and turn every experience, expected or not, into a stepping stone for forward momentum.

Authentic Leadership is not about perfection. It is about embodying the principles we've shared in this playbook. It's about making a decision and being committed to taking one small action EVERY SINGLE DAY. It's about growth and expansion, and not beating yourself up when you think that you have temporarily lost your way.

Next-Level Support For Next-Level You

Authentic Leaders don't walk alone. To sustain this journey, you must surround yourself with others who will sharpen, stretch, and support you. Build your inner circle with conscious, purposeful, intention: A coach who challenges you, mentors who check in on you, and peers who cheer you on even when your ideas seem a little wild.

Not everyone who supported you yesterday can keep pace with the speed of your growth today. Some people will fall away. That is not failure, nor judgment, it's called *evolution*. Release them with grace, and consciously create *your new team* of inspirers, challengers, and truth-tellers who will walk beside the next-level of YOU.

Authenticity Is Your Superpower

This book was written with one mission: To spark a global community of Authentic Leaders who rise together, disrupt toxic traditions, and rewrite the story of leadership.

As Rt Hon Jacinda Ardern (former Prime Minister of Aotearoa - New Zealand) said, *"Political leaders can be both empathetic and strong."*

To extend this even further, when we lead with authenticity, *Authentic Leaders* can be *both* empathetic and strong.

- Strong enough to be values-driven and make great decisions.
- Strong enough to admit mistakes and celebrate effort.
- Strong enough to listen and be moved by the people you are serving.
- Strong enough to abandon the BS and step into the present with courage.
- Strong enough to innovate with integrity, be vulnerable, and lead by example.
- *Strong enough to BE you.*

As Oscar Wilde once said: *"Be yourself, because everyone else is already taken."*

When you embrace your *uniqueness* and your *enoughness*, and consciously choose your response in every situation, you allow yourself to BE the one-of-a-kind person only you can BE!

Don't compare yourself with others. Comparison will only rob you of joy and delight. Only measure yourself against how you were yesterday, last year; before. The world doesn't need polished masks where everyone is leading the same way, the world needs YOU.

Each time you show up a little braver, a little bolder, a little more aligned than yesterday, you are living BE → DO → HAVE in its purest form.

Not someday. Not later. Not when. NOW.

You *get to choose* the timeframe. You *get to choose* your state. You *get to choose* the level of exertion/ It could be hard, it can be easy - that's up to YOU!

As you embody the learnings in this Playbook, *you get to* create ease and flow, joy and fun, impact and innovation, every single day.

The choice is yours.

The Charge Forward: Your Legacy Of Authenticity

As you will have noticed throughout this book, YOU are the example.

Every time you walk into a room, step onto a stage, or join a conversation, people notice. They feel your energy before they hear your words. You can show up weighed down by wounds and turmoil, or you can choose to rise with courage, transparency, and truth.

Every time you show up being authentic, you create the ripple of energy across the environment (and world). You give others permission to BE themselves. You show that growing, questioning, learning and taking action is the only way to BE.

Being authentic in the way you lead yourself and others (regardless of your *official* work titles), is the way of being that grows you, shapes your impact and defines your impact.

This is your legacy. Not in grand speeches or titles, but in the everyday choices to grow, to question, to lead with fire and heart. When you embody Authentic Leadership, you don't just change yourself, you transform everyone you touch.

So, go. Charge forward. BE the leader the world is aching for, and never forget ***Authenticity is your greatest superpower.***

What's Next?

As our time together in these pages draws to a close, we want to leave you with this.

- If you need permission to *be authentic,* this is it.
- If you need to know *you are enough,* this is it.
- If you need to know *how,* this is it.
- If you need to have support to *go next level,* this is it.

Step boldly into your authenticity.

Step into your power. Own the room. Redefine the rules.

YOU get to choose the type of leader you will be, no one else.

Authenticity isn't something you learn, it's *someone you choose to* BE. The greatest gift you can give yourself, your team, and the world, is the fully, empowered, authentic YOU.

Show up. Lead fully. Change everything, and have fun doing it!

Leading Forward:

What's the one quantum leap you are committing to right now that will take your being, doing, and having to the next dimension?

This is your opportunity to *live and lead* in a way that redefines everything that is possible for you, your team, and your world, forever.

Reclaim your power, take the leap, and transform your world.

About the Authors

Dr. Elizabeth Pritchard

Dr. Elizabeth Pritchard is a best-selling author, researcher, speaker, and leadership coach with over three decades of experience guiding leaders to lead authentically and with impact. Drawing on neuroscience, positive psychology, and practical coaching frameworks, she helps leaders cultivate self-awareness, resilience, and presence in high-pressure environments. In *The Authentic Leadership Playbook*, Elizabeth shares her proven strategies for turning inner clarity into external influence, empowering leaders to act with courage, integrity, and purpose.

Christine Burns

Christine Burns is a former elite athlete, CEO, and high-performance coach with over twenty years' experience helping individuals and teams unlock their full potential. Combining sports psychology with organisational strategy, she empowers leaders to step into their power, own the room, and redefine the rules. In *The Authentic Leadership Playbook*, Christine coaches athletes and leaders to own the room, move with purpose, and take courageous action that delivers real, lasting high-performance results, in business, sport, and life."

The Authentic Leadership Playbook
by **WALT Institute**

Co-founded by **Christine Burns** and **Dr Elizabeth Pritchard**, WALT Institute exists to ignite a global shift toward Authentic Leadership. We empower individuals, teams, and organizations to lead with courage, confidence, and authenticity, not through hierarchy or hustle, but through alignment, self-leadership, and purpose.

Through our **Authentic Leadership programs**, **corporate workshops**, and **high-performance coaching**, we help leaders grow their business, elevate their team's performance, and create cultures where people thrive.

Through WALT Institute, we offer three powerful ways to work with you and your team:

1. **6-Module Authentic Leadership Training** - practical, evidence-based strategies you can implement immediately.
2. **Executive Coaching** - personalised support to unlock your authentic power and elevate performance.
3. **Bespoke Training Packages** - tailored programs to transform your team, culture, and organisation.

#TALPB is more than a book - it's a movement. It's for leaders who are ready to disrupt the old rules, break free from burnout, and lead with heart. It's for individuals and teams who want to perform at their peak while staying grounded in what truly matters.

Authentic Leadership is for organizations who believe that authenticity isn't a buzzword, it's the competitive edge of the future.

Are you ready to lead differently?
Now's the time to rise, grow, and unleash your authentic power.

👉 **Connect with us:**

Dr Elizabeth Pritchard:
https://waltinstitute.com/dr-elizabeth-pritchard
https://www.linkedin.com/in/dr-elizabeth-pritchard/

Christine Burns:
https://waltinstitute.com/christine-burns
https://www.linkedin.com/in/christineburnsperformancecoach/

Bring us in for training, coaching, or bespoke programs to elevate your leadership, your team, and your organisation. Check out what we offer here: https://www.waltinstitute.com/

Socials:

https://www.facebook.com/WALTInstitute
www.linkedin.com/in/elizabethchristinewaltinstitute
https://www.instagram.com/waltinstitute/
https://twitter.com/WALTInstitute

Follow the movement and share your journey:
#TALPB #LeadAuthentically #WALTInstitute #AuthenticityRevolution

Together, we're redefining what powerful leadership looks and feels like, and it starts with you.